CUSTOMER EXPERIENCE5

18 international CX professionals
share their current best-thinking
on achieving impact and visibility
through worldclass best-practice CX

WM

Customer Experience 5

Edited by Naeem Arif and Andrew Priestley
First published in January 2024

ISBN 978-1-914265-90-7 (Pbk)
ISBN 978-1-914265-91-4 (eBk)

Contents

Welcome to Customer Experience 5

In our fast-paced and ever-evolving world, change is the only constant. As humans, we continuously push the boundaries in response to increasing knowledge and expectations.

The definition of a good customer experience is no exception. It has expanded both horizontally and vertically, with a growing acknowledgment that every industry and interaction must consider the breadth and depth of customer experience (CX). No longer confined to retail and hospitality sectors, CX is now a focal point for every business that serves customers.

As a disciple of Customer Experience, it's imperative to integrate it into every aspect of decision-making to ensure customer-centric outcomes. In today's business landscape, companies not prioritizing CX put themselves at a significant disadvantage. The best-performing companies globally owe their success to delivering exceptional customer experiences— there's no doubt about that.

Every sector should contemplate the service it provides, making the lessons shared in our Customer Experience series invaluable learning opportunities for the reader. I firmly believe that true CX practitioners are those on the frontline, engaging with customers daily. Their voices, sharing practical and innovative CX insights, need to be heard.

In our fifth edition, we're thrilled to present 18 contributions from professionals worldwide, offering their current best thinking on achieving world-class best practices.

The series' success lies in the diversity of voices represented, moving beyond the traditional consultants to include those who are actively shaping CX on the ground.

Special thanks to Andrew Priestley of WM Publishing, with whom I've now completed my seventh book project, and Ian Golding, who helped conceive this concept back in 2019. Our objective has always been to produce a high-quality series, and for this reason, we continuously seek new expert contributions from around the world.

As you read this book, keep in mind that we're already on the lookout for contributors to CX6, scheduled for release later in 2024. Feel free to connect with me on LinkedIn and express your interest in contributing to future editions.

About Naeem Arif

Naeem has three decades of experience as a retail business owner and CX consultant with specific expertise in the customer retention functions. During his time he has had the opportunity to work with senior leaders and is known for 'putting the customer first' into every solution he designs. 

As well as writing several books, he is the founder of the Customer Experience book series and can be contacted through the following social channels.

Naeem@NAConsulting.co.uk

Twitter *@NAConsultingLtd*

LinkedIn *@NaeemArif*

Facebook *@NAConsultingLtd*

8

Insights and Understandings

Insights and Understandings

Redefining Engagement:
Navigating the Era of the Machine Customers

Sirte Pihlaja

In this chapter, we delve into the intriguing realm of Machine Customers - a new horizon of CX and EX that is reshaping the very foundation of customer engagement. As organisations transition into an era where machines are not just tools but active participants in decision-making processes, understanding and catering to Machine Customers has never been more critical.

Artificial Intelligence (AI) stands as a formidable force driving transformative change, revolutionising how businesses engage with customers. It presents unparalleled prospects for personalisation, service enhancement, and fostering unwavering customer loyalty. In an age of digital acceleration and AI proliferation, organisations can no longer overlook the significance and role that Machine Customers will play in our daily lives.

But first, let us begin by demystifying the concept of Machine Customers.

By Machine Customers, I mean intelligent bots, algorithms and processes interacting on your customers' behalf to reach out to businesses independently.

These are not just cold lines of code or algorithms hidden in the background; they are intelligent entities making decisions, engaging with services, and forming their perceptions of brands.

So far, we have only scratched the surface of what Generative AI offers. Our digital representations will seamlessly interpret commands via any of our chosen interfaces, whether text, voice or video, or even deduce actions from changed patterns detected by wearables. With the introduction of AI as a core capability, Machine Customers will not need specific prompts; they'll make decisions based on the preferences of the humans they assist.

Today, using your digital assistant to browse the internet and oversee your various tasks has become exceedingly straightforward. Specialised services designed for single actions, like Amazon Dash, exist alongside community-generated code that enables your personal assistants to roam the digital realm. Alternatively, you can rely on virtual assistants such as Amazon's Alexa, which boasts compatibility with over 100,000 smart home devices (Laricchia 2022), allowing you to delegate purchase tasks via embedded Alexa skills.

This is not science fiction but a rapidly approaching reality.

As the devices and services to set up your digital assistant become more prominent and accessible, there is no limit to what regular people like you and me can delegate to our digital counterparts. A handful of specialised paid services - such as DoNotPay that can e.g. renegotiate your subscriptions and provide legal assistance to contest parking tickets (Bowder 2022) - already offer subscriptions that pave the way for a broader adoption of Machine Customers.

The Time Has Come to Revisit Automation

While you've been working hard to automate processes and implement AI strategies, primarily via machine learning-driven chatbots, your customers have been equally proactive. They've armed themselves with advanced, intelligent devices and turned the tables on automation.

While you hoped your customers would engage with the self-service portal you developed to streamline your operations and reduce costs, they've taken matters into their own hands. It has become evident that a re-evaluation of your approach is in order.

I want to illuminate why this shift in perspective is pivotal for CX and EX leaders and outline the strategic steps required to adapt and excel in this new landscape.

These digital assistants, wearables or home automation devices, and other machines can soon engage autonomously with your organisation to help humans lead healthier, less busy and more productive lives.

A machine customer is a non-human economic actor
who obtains goods and/or services in exchange for payment.
Scheibenreif & Raskino (2023)

With the help of AI, they can mimic human interactions and emulate customer behaviours. By acknowledging how Machine Customers act, we can perceive the immense value they bring to customer interactions and the magnitude of the need for the transformation they represent to modern business processes.

Machine Customers can stay on hold, waiting for a customer representative, take care of bookings, renegotiate subscriptions, dispute charges, repurchase products and services, deal with purchase orders and receipts - even make pre-emptive healthcare appointments based on following your vital statistics

- and many more recurring, preference-based, health monitoring and home or office automation activities on your customers' behalf. They can perform unexciting and time-consuming tasks that would otherwise need human attention.

No Small Change

Machine Customers are not something for the future. Today, the likes of Alexa, Google Assistant, Siri – and more recently, ChatGPT and its rivals – profoundly influence our daily lives. They've proliferated across our mobile devices, homes, cars, and business landscapes.

Remarkably, more machines are ready to function as customers than humans. Billions of IoT devices are poised and intelligent enough to assume the role of your customers. It's projected that nearly 40% of customers will experiment with utilising digital assistants to engage with customer service on their behalf by 2025 (Gartner 2022). By 2027, 50% of people in advanced economies will have AI personal assistants working for them daily (Mullen et al. 2019). In light of recent product launches, it looks pretty likely that the pace of development will only accelerate from these predictions.

From a business standpoint, Machine Customers may even be superior customers, unwavering in their reliability and commitment to making purchases. This phenomenon represents an unprecedented growth opportunity for virtually every industry.

Gartner has identified three phases in the development of Machine Customers Panetta (2023):

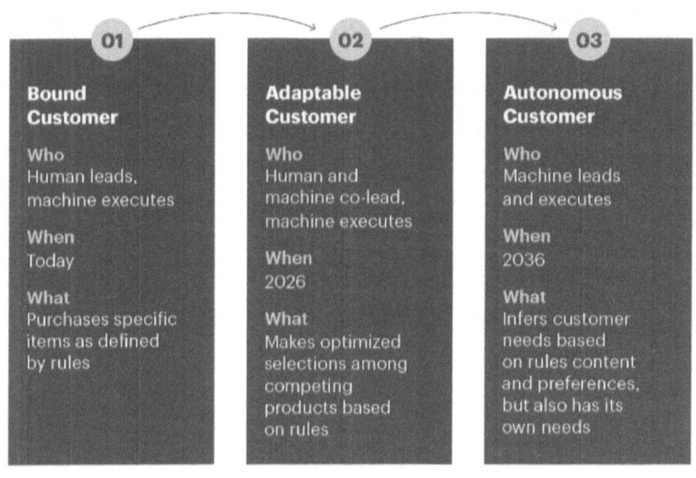

Source: Panetta 2023

1. **Bound customers** (e.g. automated re-ordering), act as "co-customers" on behalf of people, based on the rules we set for them on how to interact within a specified ecosystem, usually a single supplier

2. **Adaptable customers** (e.g. robotrading, financial roboadvisors, autonomous vehicle systems) base their behaviour on rules and some AI technology, and act with minimal human intervention, being allowed to choose between different alternatives

3. **Autonomous customers** (e.g. AI-run asset management systems) have the intelligence to act independently from their human owners

Gartner anticipates that by 2024, 100 million requests for customer service will be raised by smart products. As soon as 2026, machine customers will stand for 20% of inbound customer service contact volume. (Gartner 2023).

This transition signifies a market shift roughly twice as substantial and swift as the advent of eCommerce. A striking 49% of CEOs anticipate that the demand driven by Machine Customers will significantly impact their industry by 2030. Forward-thinking executives envision that as much as 22% of their total revenue could be derived from Machine Customers by then. (Gartner 2022)

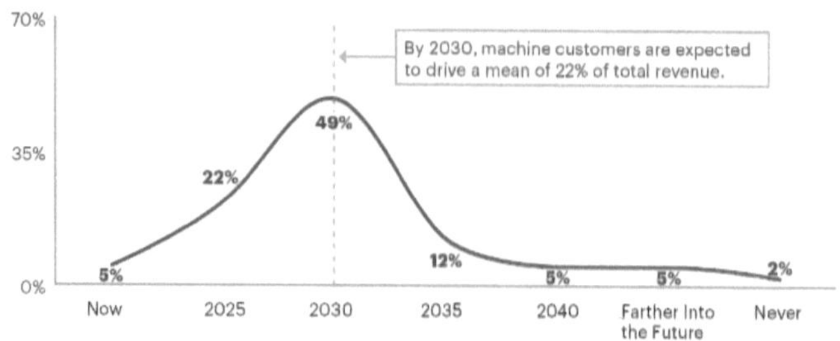

Source: Gartner (2022)

With an estimated one billion requests for customer service raised automatically by company-owned bots (ThinkCast 2022), every organisation needs to prepare for this massive emerging market. And it's not just in B2B, as virtual assistants, home automation devices and autonomous vehicles will offer a connection point to M2M commerce for B2C customers.

New potential opportunities for revenue, as well as maintaining customer relationships, are within your reach. But how do you market to a bot? You will, for sure, need to come up with novel ideas – think in terms of pitching vacant parking spaces to autonomous cars.

As OpenAI just released its GPT agents, no one has to wait for software developers or service providers to program them for us anymore. You, too, can start using a personal assistant simply by using natural language. Or, if you want to make things even easier for yourself, you can use the Humane Ai Pin, a small wearable powered by AI-based cloud services, which will do whatever you ask from it - just by talking.

Machines as Customers: The Paradigm Shift

Machine Customers do not operate within the confines of your organisation. They introduce an external layer of unpredictability and randomness to your company, mirroring the variability of human customers. The good news is that designing personalised interactions for AI-powered entities can enhance efficiency, improve accuracy, and strengthen brand loyalty.

That's because the sole objective of Machine Customers is to provide effortless experiences to their owners, and they want to solve problems as swiftly as possible. Their purchasing decisions are rooted in data-driven logic, utterly devoid of emotional influences.

Machine Customers are transparent: as logic and rule-based actors, their assumptions are visible in their decisions. They don't act on hidden intentions during the buying phase, as humans often do. They might even be more likely to commit to a supplier if the sales and fulfilment process works smoothly and simply meets the requirements of the service-level agreement. (Scheibenreif & Raskino 2023)

It's crucial to remember that machines do not have any emotions. They gather data meticulously from many sources to make informed choices based on availability, value, preferences and price. They will not forget to make purchases when running out of things. On the other hand, they will minimise waste and thus positively impact sustainability.

Understanding how Machine Customers operate is no small feat. So, all the time and effort you have put into creating better Customer Experiences based on human emotions needs to be complemented with new skills – your organisation has to master Machine Customer Experience Design.

It's not enough to merely recognise Machine Customers; decision-makers must embrace the idea of crafting tailored journeys for these virtual entities. Why? Because the very essence of CX and EX revolves around creating exceptional experiences for all stakeholders - including Machine Customers. If you genuinely want to be customer-centric, you will see their role in lowering customer effort in your business and plan accordingly to cater for your clients.

There will, essentially, be four types of customer-company interactions (Dodkins, 2022):

1. **Person-to-Person (P2P)**, the current standard as in a call to an agent

2. **Person-to-Machine (P2M)**, such as self-service and chatbots

3. **Machine-to-Person (M2P)**, when a digital assistant calls a company and talks to a person about something it has been asked to do (e.g. change a payment date)

4. **Machine-to-Machine (M2M)**, a completely autonomous, almost instantaneous encounter

Machine Customers value different things from their human counterparts on their buying journeys. It is vital that all employees in your organisation can identify when they are dealing with a Machine Customer. This is not evident, as AI-based personal assistants become increasingly difficult to distinguish from a natural person.

There is also an increased risk that bad actors may use Machine Customers to impersonate real people, leading to disruption, hacks and financial losses if organisations are unprepared to deal with them. High security must be built into business processes that handle business with Machine Customers.

Serving the Future: Your Roadmap with Machine Customers

Having given you a lot of theory, how can you now implement best practices into your organisation to deal with Machine Customers? Let me wrap up this chapter by giving you a roadmap for approaching this.

First, let's try to lay out the phases that should figure on this roadmap:

1. Form a team to start planning for the future, and involve executives to discuss your approach and strategy

2. Identify how autonomous shoppers could impact your business and the timeline for each scenario to create your Machine Customer roadmap/plan

3. Evaluate the needed skills, train and recruit and decide who owns the development

4. Start experiments to cater to Machine Customers with a minimum viable product and measure your results

5. Rinse, rewind, and repeat

Business leaders must gain a deep understanding and make strategic preparations for these sweeping changes. Start by creating a team of senior executives from sales and marketing, strategists and technologists willing to seek new opportunities outside your organisation's traditional products and markets, understand the lifetime value of connected machines and decide your role in the new ecosystem.

Do you understand what your business needs to know about planning for and dealing with this new target group? Or how will the notion of effortless customer experience change when your competitors start to deliver on this new playing field? Will your organisation be leading the pack or be left behind? (Pihlaja, 2022)

Work together with your team to draft a Machine Customer roadmap. It should be based on the scenarios where your business will interact with Machine Customers, ranked by the impact on service and cost-saving possibilities. (Dodkins 2022)

Looking at this roadmap, **evaluate scenarios and market opportunities** to formulate the new strategies or business models you will need for the future.

Consider who is in charge of and who is supporting your team facing this new breed of customer encounters. To move forward, you must define the owners for each experiment and decide who will have the overall responsibility for Machine Customer development. Is it the CEO? CIO? A Customer Experience Team? Customer Service? Or will the business departments ultimately take care of putting the action plans into practice?

Ensure your employees' well-being and envision the potential evolution of their roles. Consider the impact on Employee Experiences and identify the new tools necessary for their success. Furthermore, it's crucial to assess the additional skills that will be essential. Apart from CX teams, the need for transformation will be most drastic for the sales, marketing, data and analytics practices. Sales will become largely programmatic, and the process will be automated. Your CTO will need to build a technology landscape to support all the new business requirements.

To ready your business for an influx of Machine Customers, **revisit the needs of your customers** (and your new machine customers) in very practical terms. Follow up by defining your Machine Customers' journeys so you can manage them. Define the points of the journey where a human may need to be involved. Decide whether you should send Voice of Customer surveys to your Machine Customers, and consider how their responses may affect your results or the research questions. (...) Most importantly, talk and co-design with your customers to enable the future for lower customer effort today. (Pihlaja, 2022)

No matter what you do, **never lose sight of your human customers.** The whole point of catering to Machine Customers is to serve people better. Embracing a customer-centric approach entails persuading your organisation about the significance of your customers' digital representatives in your business and acting in their best interest. Make sure your customers get superior service, should they need or opt to interact with you. Human interaction will forever hold its value, so find the sweet spots where you can delight them.

As a CX professional, finding the right balance between the two is paramount. You must assess how increased machine interactions will shift the relationship paradigm. This endeavour demands a collective shift in our mindset.

The time has come for CX teams to fulfil these commitments, even if providing a superior customer experience might eventually translate to customers having no experience at all in the future.

Sources

- Bowder, Joshua. Announcement on Twitter (X)
  December 12, 2022.
  *(https://twitter.com/jbrowder1/5753309195?s=20&t=60ibQSBxL_
  9eSViYbVGFGA)*

- Dodkins, James. The Rise of the Machine Customers.
  November 1, 2022.
  (https://youtu.be/4l1oGSXwJ0A?si=-OTXURiFigaOoD6r)

- Gartner: Machine Customers Will Decide Who Gets Their Trillion-
  Dollar Business. Is it you? January 6, 2022. *(https://www.gartner.
  com/en/articles/machine-customers-will-decide-who-gets-their-
  trillion-dollar-business-is-it-you)*

- Gartner Says 20% of Inbound Customer Service Contact Volume
  Will Come From Machine Customers by 2026. Gartner.
  Press Release. March 1, 2023. *(https://www.gartner.com/en/
  newsroom/press-releases/2023-03-01-gartner-says-20-percent-
  of-inbound-customer-service-contact-volume-will-come-from-
  machine-customers-by-2026)*

- Laricchia, Federica. Number of Amazon Alexa compatible smart
  home devices 2017-2020. Statista. Feb 14, 2022.
  *(https://www.statista.com/statistics/912893/amazon-alexa-smart-
  home-compatible/)*

- Mullen, Anthony et al. The Future of Customer Self-Service:
  The Digital Future Will Stall Without Customer-Led Automation.
  Gartner Research. April 18, 2019.

- Panetta, Kasey. Prepare for the Future of AI-Powered Customers
  Gartner. September 12, 2023. *(https://www.gartner.com/en/
  articles/prepare-for-the-future-of-ai-powered-customers)*

- Pihlaja, Sirte. Is Your Business Ready For Machine Customers?
  November 17, 2022. *(https://www.linkedin.com/pulse/your-
  business-ready-machine-customers-sirte-pihlaja/)*

- Scheibenreif, Don. CIOs must prepare for the machine customers of the future. CIO Dive. March 27, 2023. *(https://www.ciodive.com/news/gartner-robots-customers-technology/645891/)*

- Scheibenreif, Don & Raskino, Mark. When Machines Become Customers: Ready or not, AI-enabled non-human customers are coming to your business. How you adapt will make or break your future. Gartner Inc. January 4, 2023.

- ThinkCast: What happens when your customer stops being human? June 16, 2022. *(https://youtu.be/uq8X_WIG1oc?si=sKiMlVRQYBJ0X-TY)*

- Torres, Roberto. 3 stages of machines' evolution into customers. CIO Dive. November 1, 2022. *(https://www.ciodive.com/news/machines-as-customers-AI/635399/)*

About Sirte Pihlaja

Sirte Pihlaja (Certified Customer Experience Professional CCXP & LEGO® Serious Play® Trained Facilitator) is the CEO of Shirute, the first customer experience agency in Finland. Sirte is the leader of the global Customer Experience Professionals Association's (CXPA) Finland network and was one of CXPA's founding members and a member of the International Advisory Board. She is among the first Europeans to be certified as a CCXP.

Sirte is an internationally known CX/EX expert, coach, designer and strategist with over 25 years of experience advising large international corporations and brands in different industries. She is known for translating customer understanding into concrete actions and results in a fast, fun and cost-efficient way. Sirte was recently recognised as TOP 33 Inspiring Women in CX to follow, TOP150 Global Customer Experience Thought Leader and in the CX Hall of Fame. The CXPA has also awarded her the Extra Mile Award.

Customer Experience 5 is her fourth book on people experiences. The two previous ones, Customer Experience 2 and 3, were global bestsellers on three continents.

Sirte passionately champions CX in the Nordics, Caribbean, South-East Asia and beyond and is a familiar face in international CX Awards juries and conference stages. She is especially fond of creative methodologies and regularly plays with LEGO bricks together with her clients to create a better future for all of us.

To connect with Sirte Pihlaja

Follow her on social media

LinkedIn: *linkedin.com/in/sirte*

Twitter (X): *@sirteace*

Instagram: *@sirteace*

Facebook: *www.facebook.com/shirute*

Visit websites:

www.shirute.fi/en

www.cxplay.fi

www.shirute.fi/en/cem

Insights and Understandings

Connecting the Dots from Experience Management to Value Creation and Financial Impact

Diane Magers, CCXP

As a discipline, Experience Management (including the experiences of customers, employees, partners, and brands) creates a fundamental shift in how organizations think and work. One of those shifts is the realization that employees and customers are the ultimate sources of increasing value and impact for your brand. But defining success related to creating value and financial implications for your experience practice takes more than the voice of customer and metrics reporting. We must connect the dots and link experience to actual financial impacts. Think about it – what do your executives and leaders care about? Revenue, cost, and profitability are usually at the top of the list.

Rethinking Value and Impacts

To identify and calculate the extended value and impact of experience projects, a shift in your approach to your practice is critical. This shift involves comprehensively examining impacts across the journey, service design, and viewpoints from top to bottom—encompassing customer emotions, workflows, productivity, technology utilization, and operational enhancements. Did the experience initiative reduce acquisition costs through referrals, increase sales opportunities, decrease support center calls, or shorten the time to contract? All of these aspects directly relate to financial impact. By looking at them holistically and connecting them, you create additive business value and strengthen your business case for experience changes.

Some experience management professionals specialize in crafting surveys and presenting data on metrics and correlations. While metrics like CSAT and NPS can be correlated with revenue, they don't inherently showcase specific financial impacts, unlike measurable indicators such as the number of active customers in your community or sales contacts which can be directly connected to financial impact. We must create ways that the organization and leaders can see the business critical outcomes in practical and usable terms.

Understanding Value Create and Financial Benefits

We must guide our leaders and organizations in considering value creation and financial benefits from our efforts, projects, and programs. These should encompass the diverse facets of business, human interactions, and societal activities influenced by the changes we introduce through experiences.

This approach prompts us to consider how value creation can guides our understanding of the outcomes desired by customers, employees, partners, society, and even the broader world (e.g., sustainability, trust, technological and data responsibilities, economic and ecological responsibility). What features prominently on their evaluation criteria for your brand? Are you delivering time and effort savings? In the case of businesses, how are you supporting their objectives, such as efficiency and productivity? By focusing on the element of value for customers and our organizations, you can concentrate on purposeful actions and establish critical connections to financial outcomes.

Let's start with some definitions:

- **Value creation** is the process of generating additional worth for customers, stakeholders, and society through the activities of a business or any other entity. The emphasis is on delivering products or services that meet or exceed customer expectations, addressing needs, solving problems, and providing unique or superior benefits. Examples of value creation include innovations, quality improvements, efficient processes, helping customers achieve their goals, reducing risks, and positive social and environmental impact.

- **Financial benefit and impact** refer to the gains or advantages of money or monetary resources generated due to their activities. The focus is primarily on the financial outcomes, such as revenue, profit, return on investment, cost savings, and other monetary gains. Financial benefits include increased sales, higher profit margins, cost reductions, and improved financial performance.

- **What is the relationship between value creation and financial benefits and impact?** Value creation often leads to financial benefits, as providing value to customers can increase sales, customer loyalty, and positive financial outcomes. While value creation is a broader concept that encompasses the overall positive impact generated by a business, financial benefits specifically refer to the monetary gains resulting from these activities. A successful and sustainable business ideally combines value creation and financial benefits to ensure long-term viability and positive social impacts.

Let's talk about a framework for planning through benefits realization and what you can do today to begin achieving value and financial impact through experience efforts.

A Framework for Defining, Designing, and Realizing Experience Value Creation and Financial Impact

Creating a systematic approach to value creation and financial impact involves a strategic and comprehensive process. Here's a framework and step-by-step guide to help you define and deliver the Value and Impact story for Experience Management.

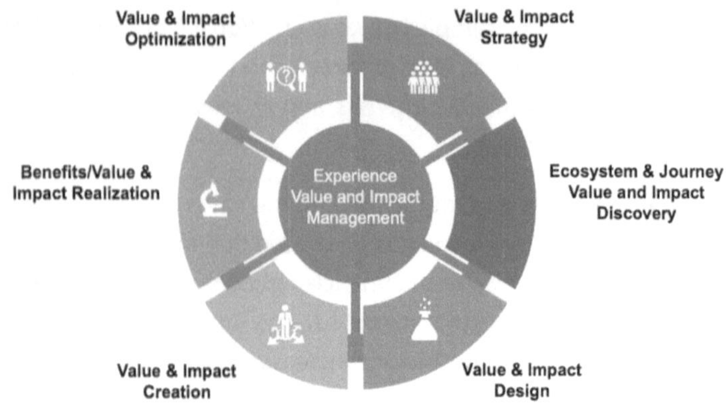

Figure 1. Experience Value and Impact Management
© Experience Catalysts, Value Creation and Financial Impact Framework, 2024.

- **Experience Value and Impact Strategy:** Clearly define the objectives and goals of how you will understand and generate value and impact.

- **Ecosystem and Journey Value and Impact Discovery:** During ecosystem and journey mapping, incorporate tools and techniques to understand where the value lies, what expectations your customers and your brand expect value, and how that is built into your ways of working.

- **Value and Impact Design:** You must purposefully design value and financial impact into your new experiences. For example, it includes measures, metrics, current and potential financial impacts, and value that can be created within your journey mapping and service design. One of my favorite questions during mapping is to ask, "What is the financial impact of this current or future experience on the organization?" and "What value can we bring to the customer, employee, partner, or our brand in this interaction."

- **Value and Impact Creation:** When you are implementing the new experiences, it's critical to ensure the right measures and metrics are in place; the teams involved understand the importance and how fostering cross-team collaboration on value and impact creation is essential to implement and realize the experience changes to achieve the targeted outcomes.

- **Benefits/Value Impact Realization:** Benefits realization refers to identifying, planning, tracking, and achieving the tangible and intangible advantages expected from a project, initiative, or experience change. It is a critical aspect of experience management that focuses on ensuring that the intended benefits are realized, and that the organization receives value from its experience investments and efforts. The goal is to move beyond the completion of activities or the delivery of outputs and to effectively capture, measure, communicate, and share the actual outcomes and benefits.

- **Value and Impact Optimization:** Optimization is the strategic and intentional effort to enhance the positive outcomes and significance derived from various experience initiatives, projects, or processes. This optimization process aims to maximize the value delivered to stakeholders and amplify the impact on the experience value and financial goals and objectives. It is critical to effectively communicate the achieved value and impact to internal and external stakeholders. It highlights success stories and demonstrates the organization's commitment to delivering meaningful outcomes through experience management.

What you can do now

I constantly hear from clients, peers and other contacts that one of the biggest challenges experience practitioners have is connecting the dots from experience management to value and financial impact. So, what can you do today, and how can you modify your approach to link actual monetary value to experience management?

Link to the executive's questions about customers, their goals, and the organization's strategic goals.

Do you know what questions leaders have, such as "Why do customers choose us? Why did they leave us? What are they saying about us? What's the impact of those activities on our success?" Do you know the measures each business unit is trying to accomplish? Knowing those goals and linking your projects to those goals to show financial impact will gain traction and support for experience management. This is the basis for creating customer and business value and generating positive financial results.

Meet with the CFO.

Gain alignment with your CFO/Finance team. Find out your organization's framework to measure and track value and financial changes. Ask for their help building a value and impact model for identifying value and impact against changes in experiences. As a bonus, helping the CFO understand the effect of Experience Management creates executive alignment.

Demonstrate that employee experience creates value and financial impact too.

Partner with your HR team to identify potential financial value for changes to the employee experience—for example, cost of acquiring talent, reducing attrition, improving productivity, etc. Bring a core team of leaders together to map the employee experience and identify where and when you can impact their experience for benefits. If you are changing the customer experience, you can bet there are benefits for the employee.

I always map the employee experience (both directly interacting with the customer and those who influence the interaction) during the discovery and design of an experience to gain potential financial and value insights).

Connect the dots for additive financial impact.

Speaking of journey mapping, it is critical to ensure you explore value and financial impacts in your mapping for financial impact. With a comprehensive view of the experience impact across the journey, you can create additive business cases that include multiple financial impacts. For example, one company I worked with optimized their Request for Proposal (RFP) approach by consolidating knowledge systems, capturing tribal knowledge, creating a virtual RFP Rapid Response team, and selecting a fantastic tech platform that helped automate their process. Some of the results were reduced systems costs (they had several knowledge management systems!), increased productivity, and a higher win rate – reflected in revenue and cost numbers. We shared those numbers with positive feedback from employees and customers and positive metrics alongside NPS, Effort Score, and Likelihood to continue the business.

Think differently about your approach to financial impact.

Here's an example of how we can think differently about measures, metrics, and value. Consider the NPS question, "How likely are you to recommend us to a friend or family member?" What if we thought about the recommendation question in a different way?

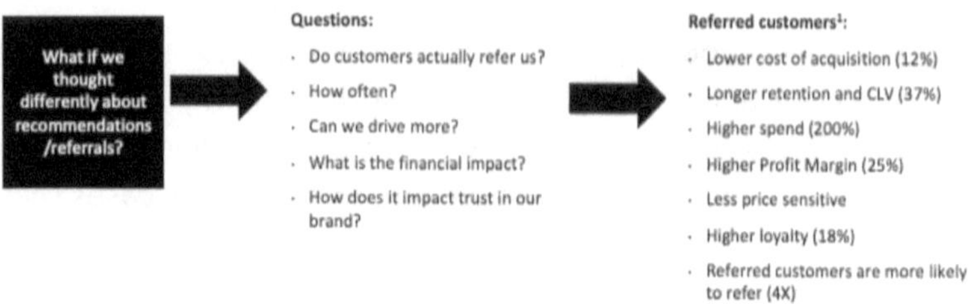

Figure 2. Example: Connecting metrics and financial outcomes
© Experience Catalysts, Value Creation and Financial Impact Framework, 2024.

Develop a value and impact strategy, plan, and structure to grow this critical activity for your practice. Clearly define how you will help customers and your organization achieve its goals. Map your activities or projects to your brand's strategic goals and each team's goals. Our role as experience professionals is to helicopter up and oversee, direct, orchestrate, and facilitate how the organization views the customer, each other, the brand, and everything they must do to drive improvement. Define the story you want to tell a year from now. What are the outcomes for your customers and you? How will you leverage the data, how will it provide value to the organization, what changes will it drive, and how will you measure it in financial terms?

Wrapping it up

I challenge you to revolutionize your Experience Management practice by adopting a comprehensive approach that reshapes how leaders and organizations perceive and engage with stakeholders. The purpose is to expand and unlock how to systematically create substantial value and financial impact for the customers and the brand. The goal is to systematically generate significant value and financial impact for both customers and the brand. This is achieved through strategic alignment of initiatives, meticulous outcome measurement, and the cultivation of a holistic understanding and realization of customer experience efforts. By ensuring success through well-planned strategies in the dynamic business landscape, organizations can optimize value creation for their customers and brands.

Sources

1. Miller, Grace. 42 Referral Marketing Statistics That Will Make You Want to Start an RAF Program Tomorrow. Retrieved December 1, 2023, from https://www.annexcloud.com/blog/42-referral-marketing-statistics-that-will-make-you-want-to-start-a-raf-program-tomorrow/

About Diane Magers, CCXP, MBA, MS

Currently the Founder and CEO of Experience Catalysts, specializing in customer and employee engagement, Diane is also Emeritus Chair and past Customer Experience Professionals Association CEO.

She is a passionate change agent laser-focused on helping brands transform experience management strategy into action and financial results.

She holds a master's in psychology and an MBA. She is a Certified Customer Experience Professional (CCXP) certified in Voice of Customer, Customer Experience Management, Net Promoter Score, and Experience Design and Innovation.

Diane Magers is an advisor, coach, and educator to experience teams as the Founder and CEO of Experience Catalysts. She is the previous CEO for the CXPA, a CCXP, CX Fellow, and co-author of Experience Rules.

Email *diane@expcatalysts.com*

Website *www.experiencecatalysts.com*

Facebook *https://www.facebook.com/diane.magers.5*

Linkedin *www.linkedin.com/in/dianemagers*

YouTube *@dianemagersccxp4905*

Insights and Understandings

The Digital Tryst:
Leveraging digital technology to enable better experiences for both employees and customers.

Nick Lygo-Baker

Why the word TRYST? According to the Oxford English Dictionary Tryst means n. An appointed meeting; n.1 confidence, faith; confident expectation, hope: = trust, n. 1,3.

In the context of Customer Experience; the meeting of Technology, Employees and Customers, creates a dynamic that is fast-moving and driven by multiple agendas. The balance of technology to human engagement has to be based on the interest of customer if it is to succeed.

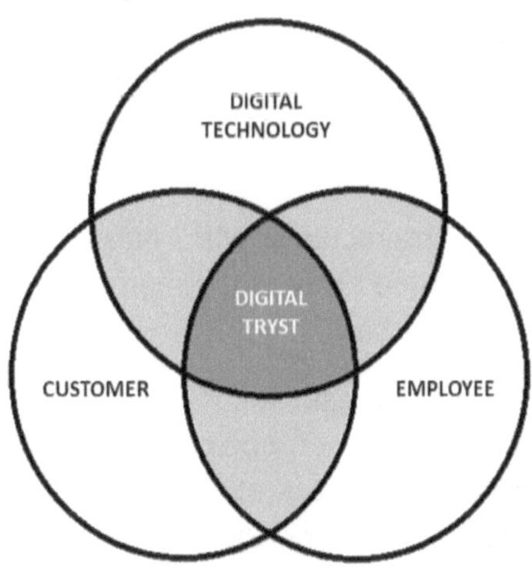

The Tryst between Customer, Employee and Digital Technology is happening regardless of whether it is intentionally designed.

This chapter looks at how to understand what makes a great experience for a customer. We can then begin to explore what employees need in order for organisations to deliver the best experience. In turn, it creates the foundation upon which technology should be built and enables the delivery of exceptional digital customer experiences every time.

The digital interactions that happen most often become the norm. That sets expectations for every other digital experience thereafter. Where these expectations are not met, people are left frustrated and disappointed.

Yet, organisations often fail to consider a unified digital, customer and employee strategy aligned with their vision and values. Those who deliberately design their customer experience can leverage the technology to enrich the lives of their customers and employees for success. Organisations must move away from just automating broken processes. Instead, technology must enhance processes and add true value to those who interact with it – whether internal (employees) or external (customers/suppliers) to the company.

The reasons to do this are simple; good use of technology in digitising processes makes it easier for customers and employees to achieve their desired outcomes. All whilst driving better engagement and ultimately loyalty with brands and organisations.

"Intense human interactions with employees create the experience that is locked away as the memory of that moment for customers– good or bad!" *

Companies need to remain focused on the customer and not be distracted by the emergence of other digital tools such as Artificial Intelligence (AI) and Robotics. The question is; Will these new technologies bridge the gap in service delivery and experience management?

To succeed digitisation must not be seen purely as a cost or time saving exercise.

AI and Robotics struggle to interpret emotion and give empathy in the same way a human does. For example, how comfortable would a patient be meeting a Virtual AI driven Doctor? Whilst it may be 100% accurate in the diagnosis? People look for sympathy, empathy and trust in the engagement with medical practitioners. After all, placing trust in a stranger at a most vulnerable time requires more than a transactional encounter.

There is no set starting point to begin a digital customer experience journey. Although a review of what Digital and Transformative Technology truly means to a Company is critical in determining how it will impact Employees and ultimately Customers!

The opportunity to succeed is there, but this needs clarity of purpose on which employees can focus and then communicate in a way that works for all stakeholders.

Unified Digital Strategy

Technology is an enabler that can be leveraged to create better outcomes. Larger organisations easily fall into the trap of creating multiple solutions for the same problem.

Teams that find themselves working in Silos tend to fix specific issues with only their own view in mind. As a result, solutions built in this way are typically limited by design and non-transferable. When a holistic and more collaborative approach is taken, solutions can be developed that better serve the wider business.

A lack of common vision at an executive level, where all leaders are aligned to a single digital strategy is a common pitfall in Digital Transformation projects. Teams are often not aligned and so end up competing instead of collaborating. This creates an environment where individuals lack trust in each other failing to work cohesively. This can be attributed to incentives which reward the wrong behaviours leading to adverse outcomes; although there can be many reasons for this situation.

The ideal scenario is when teams work together, holding each other to account. Positive conflict can be a benefit in an environment of safety and trust where everyone is working towards the same common goal.

Individuals have the opportunity to enhance their skills, benefiting the organisation as a whole. Clearly this can be difficult, but with common objectives and aligned behaviours this can be achieved.

As with any strategy whether digital or not, start with Purpose and then build back from the Customer. Mapping the customer journey, and then in parallel the employee journey, ensures alignment and understanding of what the optimal Customer Experience should look like. Only then can the business look at the technology required to enable that alignment.

Digital Technology

"Leveraging technology to achieve smarter outcomes is more than just automating existing processes!" **

Time and time again, existing processes are automated. How often do those implementing digital change thoroughly review the entire journey and evaluate the reason for digitisation in the first place?

This seems an obvious step in the design thinking process, but often, the planning does not start far enough back in the understanding of the customer decision making process. As a result, journey maps tend to be a representation of business thinking and not the view from the customers perspective.

Organisations struggle to find the balance between the right amount of technology, staff intervention and customer interaction. Digital Extremes pose a risk. Too much reliance on technology reduces empathy and the required human connection customers need in their experience with a brand. This directly affects trust and long-term loyalty.

For this reason, it is vital to understand customers and what makes a great experience. Equally, for employees – what does good feel like? By creating similar great experiences for employees, they can become genuine advocates of the brand, which carries forward into their interactions with customers.

What makes a Human Experience?

We are a lot happier with the experience of going out with friends than we are, for example, buying a new car. We love to share Experiences – this is part of how we network and connect with other people. Whereas, with products we tend to compare and contrast them. How we adapt reflects how we feel about something over time and products quickly become part of our day-to-day. For example, the thrill and excitement of that new car smell quickly becomes the norm. We adapt to products but, recall the best most exciting parts of an experience.

This recall is demonstrated in the Hedonic Adaptation model considering happiness over time below:

Hedonic Adaptation

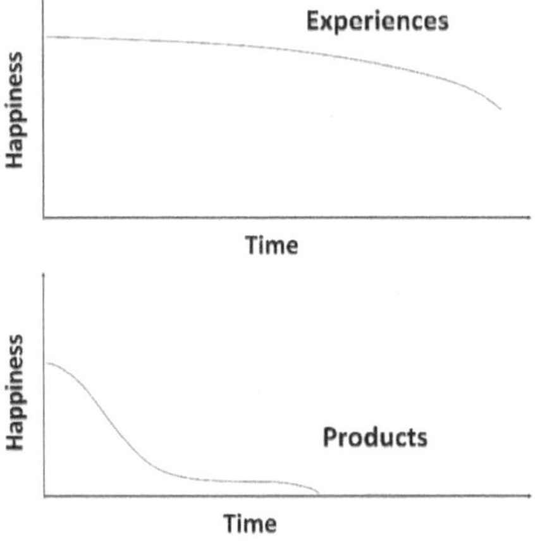

The return on investment as a business needs to deliver value. Not just in financial terms, but in terms of efficiency and ease of doing business. As technology improves, the digitisation of processes in an environment of fluid expectations places pressure on organisations. They have to consider WHY as much as WHERE technology is applied.

That is not to say we don't compare experiences or share products. According to behavioural science, our Psychology is more aligned with sharing experiences whilst, our disposition for products is more utilitarian.

Brands who operate in typically low engagement categories e.g. mobile phone provides, are creating positive experiences for their customers by offering added benefits just for being a customer. For example; a weekly coffee voucher or free cinema tickets.

The way in which we understand customer experience is changing. As we evolve the approach to journey mapping, there needs to be an equal evolution in the way customer behaviour and feedback is measured and evaluated. This in turn generates more relevant and accurate insights that better inform business decisions.

The customer journey now needs a deeper level of understanding:

Customer Marketing (Product) Journey		**Customer Experience Journey**
Customer Personas	⟶	Customer Architypes
Linear Journey Mapping	⟶	Identify "Moments that Matter" Touchpoints
Customer Service Blue Prints	⟶	Empathy Mapping
Post Event C-Sat Survey	⟶	Live "closed loop" feedback

The science of what makes a "Good Experience" is becoming more understood largely thanks to the Behavioural Scientist and Psychologist Daniel Kahneman. He worked to understand the way humans think and also how humans may react, based on their personal biases.

Kahneman's work looked at how these biases affect not only people's Implicit and Explicit responses, but their Conscious versus Unconscious thinking. Understanding how people think "system 1 and system 2" needs to be considered when designing modern customer journeys, depending on the type of experience we wish to deliver. For example, buying a drink because you're thirsty (small low consideration purchase, system 1) is very different to committing to a Mortgage (long-term expensive purchase, system 2) when making a buying decision. All of these are managing potential cognitive dissonance commonly called "Buyer's Remorse".

During 1993 in a study titled When more pain is preferred to less: adding a better end Barbara Fredrickson and Daniel Kahneman proposed The Peak-End Rule. Their model dictates that an event is not judged by the entirety of an experience, but by moments (or touchpoints) as a result of the positives or negatives in the recollection of that event.

The remembered value of touchpoints dominates the actual value of an experience. Fredrickson and Kahneman theorised that these touchpoints (Moments of Truth!) are actually the combination of the most intense points of an experience (peaks) combined with the feeling experienced at the end.

The length of time an experience takes, does not seem to have an impact on someone's retrospective evaluation. Fredrickson and Kahneman labelled this phenomenon duration neglect.

The peak–end-rule is applicable when an experience has a definite beginning and end. Moments of truth are cemented in memory based on the intensity of the experience felt at that time. Different individuals may recall an event differently as the intensity of the experience at different points create a separate viewpoint.

The application in business is clear, even with longer-term relationships between an organisation and their customer. This also applies to the organisation and their employees where a number of events and transactions with clear start-point and end-point can be managed through the Peak-End Rule to leave more positive memories.

Overlaying the Peak End Rule thinking to the Hedonic Adaptation curve, we can see the potential impact on how longer-term recollection of an experience is impacted by key moments of truth. When designing the customer journey, we could re-classify these as Moments that Matter rather than moments of truth. This helps in creating focal points when looking at what and where to invest in the customer journey.

Peak-End Rule of Experiences

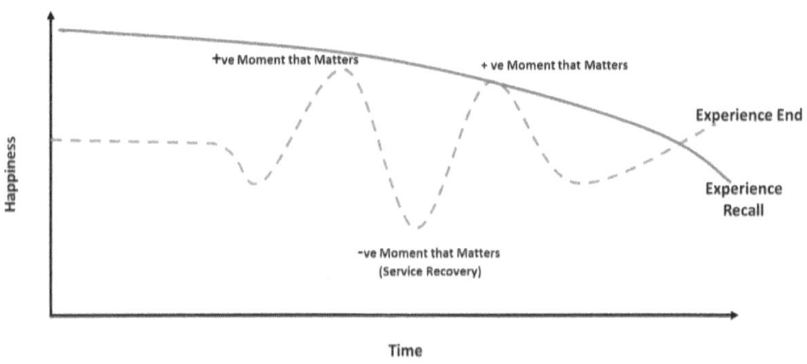

Traditional measurement and mapping processes look at every touchpoint in sequence and seek to improve efficiency at a transactional level.

Customers engaging in a digital ecosystem no longer follow a linear journey; they choose which touchpoint they wish to engage based on their specific mission. Typically, choosing to follow the path of least resistance to accomplish that mission. The store entrance, exit and the journey in between are no longer relevant in a digital journey type.

Touchpoints which can be identified as the Moments that Matter become seated in the memory of a customer. Allowing organisations to work towards managing these to the most positive outcome and, therefore the most positive recall.

Touchpoints become more optional where digital experiences occur. This differs from physical experiences as shown in this retail store journey example.

As a result, organisations are impacted by individuated consumption where customers personalise their own journey. Not all experiences are experienced the same way

The Amazon Paradox

The Amazon Paradox is where digital innovators have created a situation where expectations across industries and sectors will be the same. The digital experience provided by organisations such as Amazon, becomes the expectation of other organisation's digital experience. The way in which Amazon recommends other products, influences our expectations of other online grocery store shopping experiences.

The suggestion is that as experiences in our lives become more digital, we are more likely to compare our experiences between them. As a result, we expect the same level of experience across different providers.

Critically, when processes are delivered well by an established digital innovator such as Amazon, this sets a new minimum level of expectation. The requirement for new digital experiences from other organisations is now set at this level in the mind of the customer.

But here's the reality check! Most organisations just don't have the cash or technical ability to produce similar experiences. The likes of Amazon, Alpha, Meta and Apple have developed their digital businesses over 20+ years learning and adapting as they go.

Their common driver being the customer at the heart of their decision making.

The customer journey mapping process needs to evolve from a linear step by step process to a matrix of different touchpoints. Creates a space where customers can interact based on their specific needs, enables a more personalised journey and a better customer experience. The diagram below shows the change in behaviour across three evolving journey map examples:

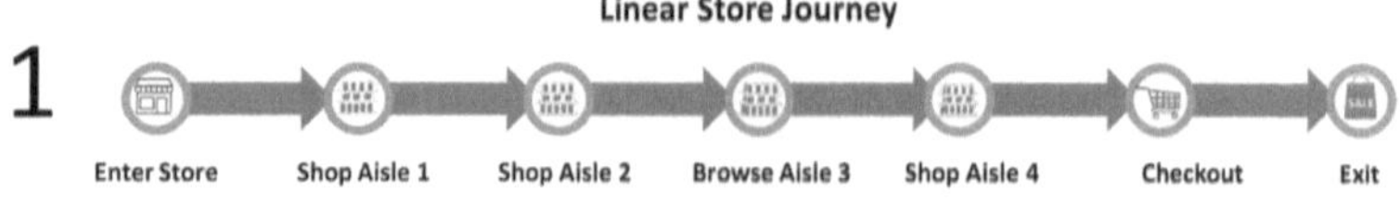

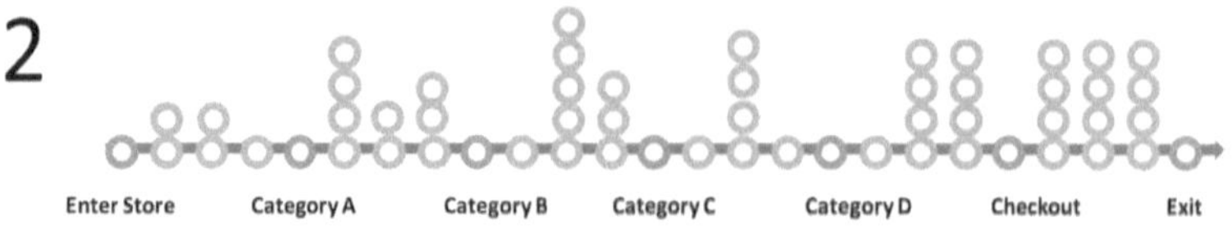

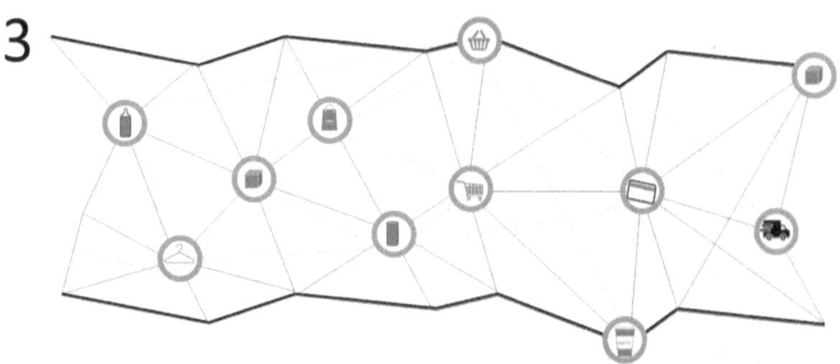

1. A linear in-store journey where the journey is prescribes irrespective of the purchase made the IKEA model

2. A more-choice driven store journey where customers visit specific categories only physical grocery store

3. A random, fully individual online journey where entry point can be store, category or at a product level.

Functional needs must be met to provide a foundation for great customer experience. This is a core requirement in delivering any digital service and ensuring every step of a journey is managed with the customer in mind. Moments of delight can only happen when moments that matter are delivered seamlessly with low effort.

Data Driving Digital

Where the focus of digital products is often on the business outcome to manage problems, leveraging the technology should be to the benefit of the employee as well as the customer needs.

The problems digital solutions solve can often be attributed to failure demand elsewhere. For example, if a manufacturing process fails and leads to an out-of-stock situation, the call centre may get additional calls as a result. By connecting more processes together digitally, we can inform both customers and employees which better manages expectations. As a result, reducing unnecessary impact (and cost) on other parts of the organisation.

Sounds simple and it is, but this level of integration requires planning, forethought and awareness to execute effectively.

Where our people make the difference

Thus far we have touched on the importance of understanding what makes a great customer experience and the impact of leveraging technology to enrich customer experiences. However, what about the people who are responsible for delivering on our brand promise?

That's right our employees, our team mates – those whose loyalty to our brand is just as important to the success of the organisation and the experience received by our customers!

Design the employee journey as part of the customer journey design process and leverage the technology to make the experience optimal for both. This approach requires organisations to begin with the customer and then the employee, before applying technology to bridge any gaps in their respective journeys. The same principles for engaging employees and building employee loyalty apply in a similar way to customers. The connection between employee experience and customer experience is not often recognised. This is driven by company structure as much as siloed thinking. Marketing typically looks after the customer and brand promise, whilst Human Resources typically look after employees.

Fluid expectations apply to employees too, by providing systems and solutions in a way which enables the employee to better serve the customer will improve business performance as a result.

The Digital Tryst

By understanding how we as humans experience technology, organisations can focus on meeting the core customer and employee needs. This enables digital solutions to drive performance improvement through enriched customer experiences.

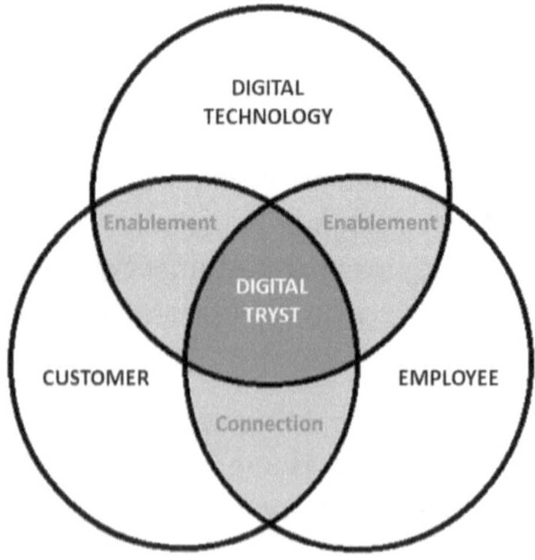

The model on p58 looks at the human connection and then technology as the enabler in the Digital Tryst.

In summary, organisations must consider technology as the enabler, not just a traditional product. By mastering the ability to adapt the digital technology to solve customer and employee problems, organisations can control the outcomes with more intention.

The result is that business should see:

- **Greater Trust**

- **Increased Purchase Frequency**

- **Deeper Brand Loyalty**

The return on digital investment needs to deliver value. Not just in financial terms, but in terms of making it easy to do business. As technology improves for everyone, the digitisation of processes in an environment of fluid expectations places pressure on organisations to consider **WHY** and not just Where technology should be applied.

Sources & References:

Quotes

- *View on what in an experience triggers a memory during human interaction – Nick Lygo-Baker © 2024

- **View on approach to use of technology to improve customer experience – Nick Lygo-Baker © 2024

Hedonic Adaptation

- Philip Brickman and Donald T. Campbell coined the term in their essay "Hedonic Relativism and Planning the Good Society" (1971)

- Well-Being: Foundations of Hedonic Psychology edited by Daniel Kahneman, Edward Diener, Norbert Schwarz

- Seunghwan Lee and Dae-Young Kim , "The effect of hedonic and utilitarian values on satisfaction and loyalty of Airbnb users"- 2017

- Thomas Gilovich, Amit Kumar, in Advances in Experimental Social Psychology, 2015

- Christina Armenta, Nattavudh Powdthavee, Alois Stutzer Kennon M. Sheldon, in Stability of Happiness, 2014

- Elizabeth W. Dunn, … Lara B. Aknin, in Advances in Experimental Social Psychology, 2020

Peak-End Rule

- Kahneman, Fredrickson, Schreiber and Redelmeier. "When More Pain Is Preferred to Less: Adding a Better End" 1993.

- Tryst - Meaning Definition - Oxford English Dictionary www.oed.com c1425- and c1200-1483

About Nick Lygo-Baker

Nick is an experienced leader in customer experience strategy insight and digital transformation. He has been listed in the top 25 CX influencers and top 25 CX Practitioners by CX Magazine and top 150 Global Influencers and Thought Leaders by SurveySensum.

As both a Certified Customer Experience Professional and a Certified Member of the Market Research Society, Nick has been helping organisations measure and improve their customer experience for almost 20 years.

He has held global leadership roles within some of the worlds' top Customer Research Organisations. More recently Nick has acted as a virtual-CXO within Retail, Hospitality sectors providing hands on guidance for organisations looking to improve their Customer Experience.

A millennial Retail graduate, Nick's experience covers a broad range of B2C and B2B industries (including Retail, Hospitality, Financial Services, Pharma, Automotive and Public Sector) designing some of the most innovative and engaging Customer Experience Strategies underpinned by purposeful Feedback, Insight and Data Solutions.

LinkedIn *www.linkedin.com/in/nlygo-baker*

Insights and Understandings

Leadership In Customer Experience

Hamdi Al-Amawi

Can Experience Beat Product and Service?

I remember I used to visit a restaurant with my family in one of the countries I used to work in.

We always had other options, but this restaurant was always our number one choice.

The food was good (not excellent) but the people working there were amazing, they were very friendly, helpful and always smiling in a way that felt sincere.

On one occasion whilst dining there with my wife, I remember whispering to her: "the soup is not very hot". This was whilst the waiter was engaged in putting the dishes on the table. When the waiter returned, he surprised us by bringing another dish of hot soup with an apology. We had not complained to him, he had just overheard our whispers! Following this, the restaurant manager also came and offered his apologies.

After this, I took time to reflect on this short but interesting experience. What made the waiter act the way he did?

How did the restaurant management succeed in instilling this customer- centered attitude in the employees? The answer came immediately to my mind "If the manager himself came and apologized then expect the employee to do more than this".

What I want to share from this experience is that customers are not only concerned about the product, but they are also concerned about how they are treated by our employees; they have become much more emotionally driven and I believe this is now becoming more important than the product itself. (especially after COVID19).

Customer Experience Is Everybody's Responsibility In The Organization

I spent over ten years in DHL Express in Saudi Arabia and Bahrain. During my time, I remember a specific customer: A gentleman who told us that his daughter is getting married in two days. Unfortunately, the wedding dress, which he customized for his daughter was torn upon delivery by one of the courier companies. It took him six months to customize this wedding dress and now he was worried that the torn wedding dress could ruin this momentous occasion, both for him and for his daughter.

The customer called us seeking help to ship the dress back to the designer to fix the dress. The lead-time would take two days to send the dress to Italy where it would be fixed. It would then take another two days to return it and by that time, the wedding would already be over!

One of our senior management team suggested booking a ticket and flying with the dress carrying it by hand, he also he suggested sending pictures of the torn dress to the designer in advance so that they could better prepare to fix the dress, especially if it meant sourcing additional materials.

A flight booking was made, and the senior manager took the responsibility of traveling to manage the reparation of the dress. When he arrived in Italy, the dress was fixed on the same day. The senior manager came back to Saudi Arabia on the morning of the wedding and delivered the dress to the customer.

Mission Accomplished, you cannot imagine how happy the customer was to receive this dress.

Delivering exceptional customer experience is everybody's responsibility in the organization. Creating a culture of "the customer is at the heart of everything we do" must be one of the tops of leaders' concerns and responsibilities in any organization who seeks to excel in providing a great customer experience to its customers.

When I started my career as a frontline agent in a large telecommunication company, I used to answer over one hundred calls every day.

One day I was on a call with an angry customer when suddenly the commercial manager came in and sat next to me.

I was new at that time and the call was not perfect. After I finished the call, we discussed the call scenario and he explained to me what things could have been done to make the call better. He asked me if he could take the next call, he answered the call and focused on what we discussed in my call. I really liked his on- job coaching approach with me to develop my skills in answering customers' calls and inquiries; it was really a great experience to me with one of the senior management staff, which had a positive impact on my performance in answering customers' calls and inquiries.

The key takeaways from my previous examples are to emphasize the importance of leadership in Customer Experience, which is very crucial for organizations in this customer driven business environment to compete and stand out among the crowd.

The Crucial Role Of leadership in Customer Experience

Here are some useful insights about the importance of leadership role in creating a customer centricity culture and implementing a great customer experience strategy in the organization:

Leading by Example

Leading by example is the best way to instill and spread the customer centric values among the employees, exactly like the previous experiences I have explained where the top management was involved and engaged in creating a positive customer centricity environment.

It will motivate the employees to empathize with customers and set the standard for how employees should interact with the customers through active listening and commitment to helping customers and solving the customers' issues proactively without waiting for them to complain.

Empathy is at the Top of the Organization Core Values

Business leaders should put empathy in top priority as a core value in customer journey mapping, encouraging employees to try to understand customers mind set and emotions to respond quickly and proactively which will always not only create a positive impact on the customer experience but may also improve the quality of customers' lives.

Cross-Functional Teamwork

It is the business leaders' responsibility to harmonize and align different departments and functions efforts towards the customer centricity to build and emphasize this culture among the organization from the top to the bottom, regardless of the function or the department in the organizational structure, which will eventually result in a seamless customer experience journey.

Cultural Considerations

This is a very critical concern relates to the culture in which business leaders must pay attention when mapping the customer journey strategy, especially when operating internationally, what fits here may not fit there and what is good here may not be good there.

Euro Disney is a clear example when they operated in Paris and failed to consider the cultural differences, which eventually resulted in failing to create a great customer experience in the park.

Leaders Engagement in Customer Experience Strategy

Investing in Customer Experience is very crucial for business leaders in adopting it and approving customer experience strategy, but will this be good enough to create a great customer experience in the organization?

For organizations to succeed in implementing the customer experience strategy, it is very important for leaders to engage and involve in setting and implementing this strategy.

Cascading the strategy must come from the top to the bottom and everybody in the organization should be involved and engaged in implementation with the leaders' supervision and follow up with different functions and department heads.

Employee Experience

Employee experience is very crucial in creating a great and consistent customer experience; happy employees will always end up with happy customers.

Employee experience can influence customer experience in different ways some of these ways and approaches are:

Training and Development

Business leaders must focus on training the employees on products and services and developing their skills, well-trained and knowledgeable employees will enable them to be experts in problem solving and answering customers' inquiries and concerns proactively.

Employee Empowerment

It is not good enough to train the employees on how to deliver exceptional customer experience; leaders who believe that customer experience has a great positive impact on the business should also empower the employees and provide supportive environment to deliver exceptional customer experience and go the extra mile when resolving customers' issues and complaints.

Employee Feedback (Voice of the Employee)

It is very important for business leaders to give the opportunity for employees to express their insights and suggestions, especially when it comes to front liners who are in direct communication and interaction with customers.

You might have the best product or service suggested and designed by front liners, rather than what resulted from research and development department, because of their understanding of customers' needs and preferences, and the relationship they build everyday with the customers, they are the best who can know your customers and their preferences and put your product design on the right way to offer it to your customers.

Employee Engagement

Creating a positive and engaged work environment is one of the most important factors and responsibilities for business leaders to enforce in the organization, this can be through effective communication, recognitions and appreciations, town hall meetings, team building.

Motivated and engaged employees will create a highly committed, satisfied and productive team, which will definitely have a positive impact on the quality of customer experience.

Ken Allen former CEO of DHL Express had a very successful story in taking the company from losses for so many years to become one of the best service provider and profitable company in the world by improving the employee experience through creating and enforcing a positive work environment, training and focusing on employees' engagement.

He initiated a global world-class training program for 100000 employees based on a customer centric vision to instill the customer centricity and customer focus culture in the company globally, the training focused on four pillars based on Customer Focus, International Knowledge, Global Network and Responsibility.

Ken had succeeded in his initiative through engaging everybody in the organization from the top to the bottom in mapping the customer experience journey.

Summary

It is very evident that Customer Experience is now not a choice rather than a necessity in the organizations, since products and services are now similar and not the only reason that makes customers buy and interact with the company; it is time now for business leaders to think differently from customer experience importance and positive impact perspectives.

Leadership in Customer Experience Is absolutely crucial in any organization who seeks to thrive in this very highly customer driven and competitive business environment. Human Centricity (Employees and Customers) will always create a great customer experience.

It always starts with setting a customer centric vision to leading by example and empowering and engaging employees, building a positive cross-functional work environment, prioritizing the customer experience and putting the customer at the heart of everything that company does to deliver an exceptional customer experience.

Prioritizing customer experience in organizations will not only have a positive impact on customers but also will grow the organization revenue. It is evident for business leaders that customer experience is not only a supportive function in the organization but also it is an effective way of generating revenue, through customer acquisition, customer retention, increase customer lifetime value and cost reduction.

About Hamdi Al-Amawi

Hamdi Al-Amawi MBA, CECP is a dedicated CX professional with a passion for human centricity of employees and customers, for delivering exceptional customer experience.

Hamdi has more than 20 years of experience working in different industries in retail, manufacturing, aviation, telecoms and logistics - with an outstanding record of success and a deep commitment to creating and driving revenue and continuous improvement of businesses in challenging customer-driven markets. He strongly believes that CX is not a function or only a business strategy in organizations but also a way of improving people's quality of life. Hamdi is a Gulf CX Awards Judge (2019-2023) and Customer Centricity World Series Awards Judge. He is currently a Doctor of Business Administration candidate. His main areas of expertise are service excellence, strategy, continuous improvement, employee engagement and morale resource, consulting and training.

LinkedIn *www.linkedin.com/in/hamdi-amawi-91176232*

Insights & Understandings

Customer Experience in Finance Processes

Philip Rürup

Introduction

You have probably heard stories of people who inherited a house, and then, to their surprise, behind a locked door covered in cobwebs, they discover a valuable painting or a rare, well-preserved old timer in the garage. What if I told you that from a Customer Experience perspective, there are corners in your business that offer this kind of unexpected, untapped potential?

In this chapter, we will explore one of these corners. There is a good chance you will discover a topic to which you've previously given little or no attention: the administrative parts of the customer journey, particularly the finance processes. You will realize that even in this area, the beauty and effectiveness of Customer Experience present significant opportunities, and I will provide you with some impulses to start unlocking this potential.

However, before you continue reading, you must be willing to be thrown back in time to the 1990s in terms of CX's progress. Ready?

Here it goes.

The Jekyll & Hyde Effect of Customer Experience

The topic we will examine together is customer-facing finance processes. While nearly every company has initiated the Customer Experience transformation, the initiatives have focused mostly on winning and serving the customer. Meanwhile, the finance processes, from invoicing to collections, have been almost entirely neglected. Their Customer Experience ranges from neutral to terrible. At troy, we call this the Jekyll & Hyde effect of Customer Experience.

The Jekyll & Hyde Effect of Customer Experience

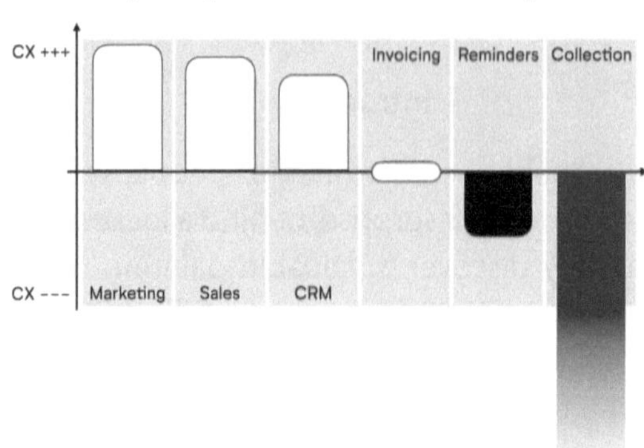

The Relevance of Finance Processes

When we consider the relevance of these processes for the end-to-end Customer Experience, this oversight seems critical because finance processes account for a high share of customer touchpoints. Typically, customers receive invoices for every purchase. On average, about 20% of customers pay late[1] and receive up to five payment reminders before being handed over to external debt collection. 2% to 4% of customers receive the "intensive care" of debt collection, sometimes with dozens of touchpoints before eventual payment.

When you add the related inbound contacts, these processes represent one of the most important interfaces to your customers. This is enough reason to examine why the Finance Experience hasn't been prioritized until now.

Why do Finance Processes get neglected?

My team and I have heard many excuses for the omittance of finance processes. Frequently, companies argue that regulatory obligations are too strict to allow for a more positive experience. In reality, these legal requirements are hardly more extensive than those for marketing or sales communication, but the discourse about balancing them with CX considerations has never taken place.

Status Quo: Who determines the Content Design?

When discussing the poor status of the arrears management, the standard justification is that customers who don't pay on time are not worth preserving. If you consider that 60% of customers simply forget to make timely payments or face temporary liquidity shortfalls[1], this reasoning is not tenable.

An explanation that might be closer to the truth but also harder to face is the general tendency to overlook finance processes in transformation projects. For instance, finance processes remain notably undigitalized to this day. According to an EOS study, only 50% of financial decision-makers consider their reminder processes digitized.[2]

This might even be wishful thinking because, according to HFS Research, 85% of operational finance managers rate their organization's digitalization progress as insufficient.

The lack of digitalization arises because the C-Suite questions the potential of finance processes both regarding use cases and an expected return on investment[3], again in stark contrast to the operation managers' assessment. According to Gartner, there is no other department where the view on potential optimization is so polarized.

And it gets even worse: When decision-makers were asked why budgets to digitalize the finance processes were declined, the second-most frequent answer was "The inertia of finance managers."[3] With this kind of prejudice, it is no surprise that finance departments lag years behind other divisions in digitalization and CX transformation.

Finance Experience - A moral Obligation and a unique Opportunity!

However, this bleak status quo has a silver lining: any effort to improve the Finance Experience will pay off multifold. On top of catching up with other departments and changing the prejudices about laggard finance professionals, there are many more reasons to tackle it.

1. Moral purpose

The first aspect is a moral imperative. Today's finance processes with complicated wording, visually challenging design, and poor processes are difficult to understand and fully digest. This is true for anyone in a stressful situation, but even more so for people who struggle with language anyhow. It is vital to consider that, statistically, 10% to 20% of the global population

- independently from economic or ethnic backgrounds - suffer from dyslexia[4], 15% to 20% show symptoms of language-based learning disabilities[5], and 25% of adults have reading skills on an elementary school level.[6] If you factor in that the top three complaints about reminder processes are missing context, feeling unsettled by the process, and feeling ashamed, it becomes apparent that applying our Customer Experience toolbox is a moral necessity. Improving the Finance Experience will allow everyone to understand their financial obligations better and make it easier to attend to them.

2. Customer delight

Secondly, the low bar of customer expectations allows even to delight customers. For invoices, customers expect nothing more than an accounting document since well-executed e-invoicing remains a rarity. For payment reminders, the current standard is lawyer-drafted letters that look like they were printed with a dot-matrix printer. And in debt collection, customers assume even worse.

Formula for Customer Delight

Execution - Expectation = Delight

With reasonable optimization, you can surpass customer expectations, resulting in measurable benefits. You should be able to generate top ratings in Customer Satisfaction Surveys and turn customers into promoters in NPS Surveys.

For example, in the projects we have supported to optimize the Finance Experience for debt collection processes, we typically use a targeted survey to evaluate satisfaction with this stage of arrears management. In a digital survey, we ask customers six questions about their satisfaction with the support, the communication's clarity, the web portal's helpfulness, etc.

High Customer Satisfaction even with Late Stage Collections

In these projects, we have measured an average satisfaction score of 4.3 of 5 stars. Remember that this feedback rates satisfaction with a debt collection process, where the product is treating customers well while collecting their money. With this scope, such satisfaction can be considered an excellent result. Even more delightful is that 50% of customers rate the process with a "perfect score", answering all six questions with 5 stars. This proves customer delight is possible - even in processes like debt collection.

3. Employee delight

Suppose you achieve this degree of customer satisfaction. In that case, it is also not uncommon that customers even take the time to express their satisfaction in writing, e.g., by sending emails with appraisals. Imagine the atmosphere in your early arrears team when, instead of hearing complaints and excuses, they start receiving compliments. You can enhance this effect by sharing customer compliments with the entire division on an anonymized basis. This creates a self-reinforcing effect of positive emotions that lead to better customer service, resulting in more compliments, etc. We have witnessed a positive impact on all sorts of HR key performance indicators, like a stronger sense of purpose, better employee Net Promotor Scores, higher productivity, improved sickness rates, and reduced employee churn.

High Employee Net Promoter Score

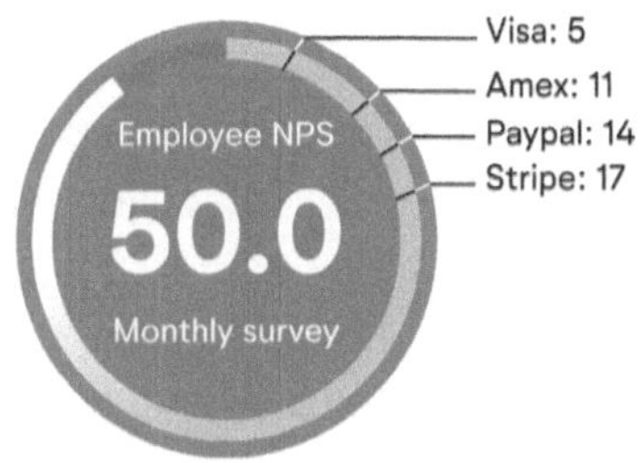

Reduction of Sickness Rates

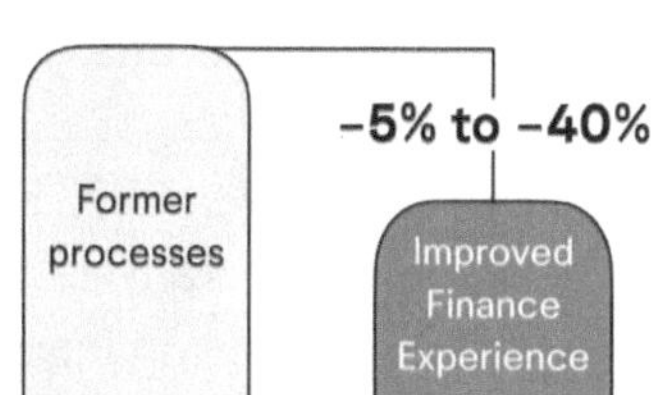

4. CFO delight

Should you still decide whether to pursue or advocate enhancing finance processes, I can provide you with one last argument. An improved Finance Experience doesn't compromise payment rates but, in fact, bolsters them.

Accelerated Payments strengthen Liquidity

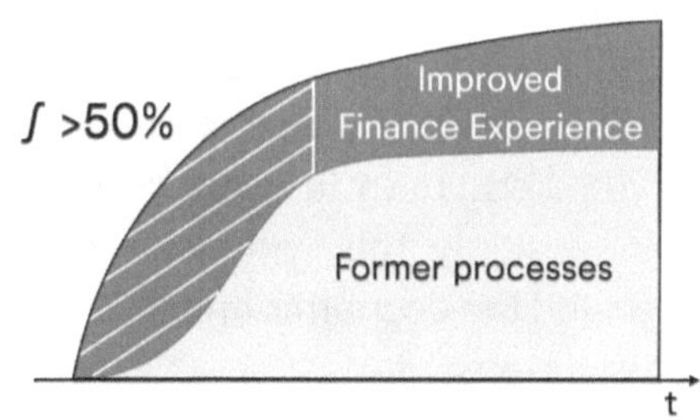

In projects across nearly any industry, we have measured a significant acceleration in customer payments. As an example from a leading e-commerce company, we were able to optimize finance communication and the late-payment self-service portal, resulting in a 50% increase in cumulative payments in the first four months after the due date. This effect strengthened the liquidity of our client meaningfully. As a logical consequence, fewer customers fall seriously behind and never reach rather unpleasant stages like judicial collections, which, in turn, improves customer satisfaction.

If the Invoice-to-Cash processes are optimized end to end, including external debt collection, we have also witnessed significant improvement in the total payment rates, thereby reducing debt write-offs. In benchmark to more traditional debt collection processes, we have measured uplift of collection rates by 10% to even 80%. Keep in mind that a reduction of debt write-offs linearly translates to increased profitability, so even a 10% improvement can lead to 6- to 8-digit savings annually.

Significant Improvement of Payment Rates

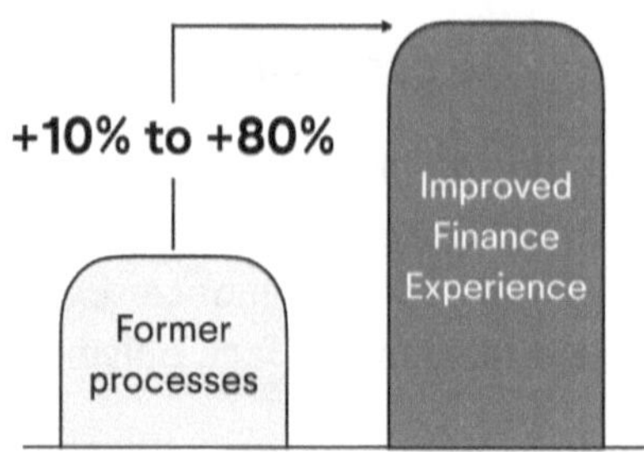

Lastly, the combination of higher customer satisfaction, quicker payment, and improved payment rates should help preserve many thousands of valuable customer relationships. We have seen reduced churn in these processes by as much as 75% to 80%. Multiply this with your standard customer acquisition costs, and the economic impact can even exceed the savings in debt write-offs.

Finance Experience - how to get started

For Customer Experience professionals, the necessary ToDos will be rather obvious once you start analyzing today's communication and processes.

If you are a Finance Professional, you might appreciate some impulses about where to start. I suggest starting with the fundamentals of your Invoice-to-Cash outbound communication, the letters, emails, Messenger texts, etc.

Simplify wording and layout

Simplify the wording using A2 to B1 language level vocabulary, keep sentences short, and avoid lawyer terminology wherever possible. It is also advisable to consider language-specific reading patterns (e.g., F- or Z-Shape for Latin script) to position essential elements along the axes people focus on when scanning texts. Use bold print, colors, and icons to guide the readers' attention.

Reading-/Perception Patterns in Latin Script

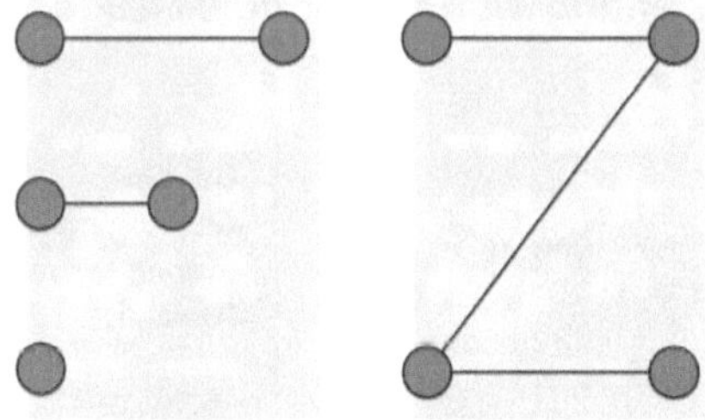

Be bold and use emotions

One of my favorite studies, a Qualtrics survey about the relevance of emotions in Customer Experience, revealed something groundbreaking: As it turns out, nothing is more important to today's customers than having an emotionally pleasant experience. This is even more critical to them than whether their issue was resolved or how much effort they had to exert.

The Importance of Emotions

	Issue resolved	Effort to resolve	Emotionally pleasant
Likely to trust the company	76 %	78 %	85 %
Likely to purchase again	83 %	84 %	90 %
Likely to recommend	81 %	83 %	90 %
Likely to forgive a struggle	62 %	64 %	74 %

Qualtrics Consumer Benchmark Study Q2 2020

Even in the Finance Experience, it's possible to incorporate emotional elements. This can be done, for example, by using imagery in emails or on landing pages. Here are a few ideas, but remember that the images and tone of voice must align with your brand identity. Your marketing colleagues can assist in this.

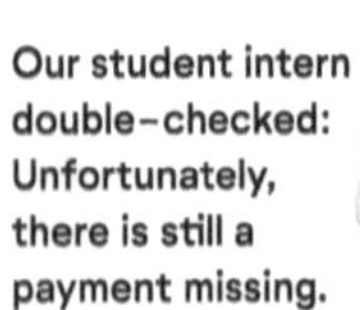

Naturally, textual elements can also evoke emotion. To spark your imagination, let me give you a few examples. For a first-time order invoice, you could say, "The entire XYZ team is thrilled to welcome you as our customer!"

If a customer places frequent orders, it could read, "We're honored that you've once again placed your trust in us."

Behavioral Economics

As a theoretical framework that can help you choose the best wording and imagery, I recommend behavioral economics, particularly the sub-discipline of cognitive automatic responses. In the literature, these responses are often pithily phrased as biases, which makes them quite easy to utilize. For example, people are more responsive to personalized communication, so you might want to use full names for the addressee and sender, use "I" and "we" in the text, and possibly even include a photo of your service center director.

Another example would be that individuals feel they behave correctly if they act like others ("social proof"). You could use this in an invoice to overcome the post-purchase dissonance by saying, "You made the right decision, just like 9 million other satisfied customers." On a digital payment page, you could use this bias to guide people to a preferred amount in the installment feature. "90% of customers in your area/your age group/... choose a monthly installment of XX."

The Indispensability of Success Measurement

I'd like to close by encouraging you to approach optimizing the Finance Experience experimentally and data-driven. If you introduce optimization step-by-step with A/B testing, you can prove the effectiveness of some changes while disproving others. Particularly regarding topics as subjective as wording or imagery, this way of objectifying the improvements will allow for sustainable and replicable results. Early, measurable success will motivate you and your team to continue this path, and hard KPIs will help communicate the improvements to your senior management to overcome the prevailing prejudices.

Let me know how it goes :)

References

1. EOS Study "European Payment Practices 2019"

2. EOS Survey "European Payment Practices 2022"

3. HFS research, 2020

4. Wu Y, Cheng Y, Yang X, Yu W, and Wan Y (2022) Dyslexia: A Bibliometric and Visualization Analysis. Front. Public Health 10:915053. doi: 10.3389/fpubh.2022.915053

5. Dyslexia Center of Utah

6. Cross River Therapy

- Graphics 1, 2, 4 - 11: © troy gmbh 2023

- Graphic 12 Content © Qualtrics 2020, Visualization © troy gmbh 2023

- Graphics 3, 13 - 15 Photos © Adobe Stock, Text © troy gmbh 2023

About Philip Rürup

Philip Rürup is a serial entrepreneur and a pioneer in the field of "Finance Experience" - the application of customer experience principles in finance processes. With a foundation in a traditional corporate career at Arvato/Bertelsmann, Germany, until 2016, Philip's expertise spans financial services, marketing, and data management.

He co-founded Yes.com aiming to revolutionize identity verification in banking. In 2018, he established troy, heralded as the world's "friendliest debt collection company," with friendliness as a synonym for tech-driven customer experience. troy's SaaS solutions and end-to-end services have redefined Finance Experience, earning it multiple accolades, including two gold iCXA® awards in 2021 and three gold DACH CXA® awards in 2022. Recognized as a global customer experience leader in debt collection by an extensive survey, troy continues to set new industry standards that can be applied to all stages of invoice-to-cash processes.

Email *philip@troy.de*

LinkedIn *www.linkedin.com/in/philipruerup/*

Website *www.troy.de*

CX Strategy

CX Strategy

Six Ways In Which Results Driven Organisations Achieve CX Excellence

Scott Lee Holloway

Whilst organisations may not all realise it, they are all delivering a customer experience. Needless to say, each organisation will be at a different maturity level when it comes to its customer experience management (CXM). With over a decade of experience in financial services, I have seen a lot and learned a great deal through a number of projects and initiatives to which I have directly contributed.

In this chapter, I am going to provide guidance drawing upon my experience, to help organisations know where to start. Your organisation may be on the back foot or behind the curve when it comes to CX. Well, the good news is that it's never too late to start defining your organisation's desired customer experience and, crucially, embedding that into the fibre of everything you're doing. I will share my top six tips on the best ways to get started. After all, a journey of a thousand miles begins with a single step!

Wherever your organisation is on its CX journey, and however advanced your CX efforts may be, you are never starting with a blank slate. I often liken it to a jigsaw puzzle. Organisations often have many of the required pieces for CX success. It's a matter of bringing it all together in unison and filling in any gaps. This is where CX professionals add immense value to organisations, in viewing matters through a uniquely customer-centred, holistic lens. We need all employees to be ambassadors of our organisation and to care deeply about all aspects of the business, not just the parts they are directly responsible for. Start with what data you have available, and your complaints register is your best friend in this regard! This will give you a clear picture of any areas driving customer dissatisfaction and help you identify recurring customer pain points. Then, you can formulate strategies and recommendations to address them.

It's also vital to acknowledge the intrinsic connection between Employee Experience (EX), and Customer Experience (CX), which fuse to represent the Human Experience (HX).

Business is all about understanding people, your own people, your customers, and other stakeholders. You must avoid honing in exclusively on your customers' needs and also pay attention to your colleagues' needs, also known as your 'internal customers'. Put simply, your people will treat your customers in the same spirit as they are treated. Therefore, to deliver the desired customer experience your organisation wants for its customers, you need to ensure that you have a team of engaged, empowered individuals working in unity towards the organisation's shared aims and objectives.

When starting out, I focused as much of our efforts on working with our internal customers (our colleagues), as I did on improving aspects of the customer journeys for external customers. It's essential to bring your colleagues along as you embark on your journey toward CX Excellence. Outline what the organisation is setting out to achieve, and make sure that what you need from them and their role in delivering the desired outcomes is clear.

Drawing upon my experience of working in high-performing organisations, here are my top six tips to get the best structure and customer-centric culture:

1. **Secure leadership buy-in.** Obtaining leadership buy-in is crucial in securing universal support across the organisation. I apply a top-down, bottom-up approach. Start with the leadership team, and ensure that they 'get' the vision and authentically understand the value of delivering an exceptional customer experience and the connection between customer satisfaction and bottom-line performance. To gain momentum, I started with a CX maturity assessment workshop with our C-Suite to measure our maturity in customer experience and obtain our senior leaders' support. Once you've crossed this bridge, you can then work on imparting the shared vision across all levels of the organisational structure.

2. **Be data-driven and purpose-led.** It's vital to be led by your organisation's purpose. However, it's crucial to do so in an informed manner. As previously mentioned, utilise any available insight, and where there is any missing data, work to gather it. Check in with your customers regularly to ensure you understand their needs and expectations. Doing so will enable you to

effectively prioritise your optimisation efforts toward the areas where they will be most impactful. We deploy many methods to conduct pulse checks with our customers and focus equally on the structured feedback loops (such as CSAT surveys, focus groups, and mystery shopping exercises) and the unstructured feedback loops (complaints and feedback that our customers have freely volunteered). The magic happens when you combine these two sources of insight and leverage them in tandem as part of your continual improvement processes.

3. **Recognise colleagues.** Wherever you are able to, reward colleagues for role-modelling the behaviours the organisation wants to see. For example, we introduced Feedback Terminals across our branch network and a quarterly reward scheme to recognise the excellent results and glowing customer feedback captured via this initiative. It's essential not only to reward the highest performance, but also to recognise those who have made the most significant efforts to improve, regardless of where they are positioned on the leaderboard. Also, don't be afraid to make it fun! The more engaging you make the topic, the more it will resonate, and the messages you wish to impart will 'land'. Continual coaching and dedicated training efforts are crucial to achieving this aim. I'm a big believer in gamification. For instance, as part of our CX training efforts, I deployed the Lego serious play methodology as a training aid, which our colleagues wholeheartedly embraced. We also filmed and released a James Bond-style movie trailer when introducing a new complaints management tool. The trailer cost very little, requiring creativity and 'outside the box' thinking. However, it created a phenomenal level of engagement and ensured the new system launched with a 'splash'.

4. **Continuous growth.** The world of CX is constantly evolving, and as CX professionals, we must embrace a growth mindset and never stop learning. Staying abreast of best practices and developments across the field is essential, and I ensure that I dedicate time to attending courses, workshops, and seminars on a regular basis.

An achievement I am proud of is that I became my country's (Malta) first-ever Certified Customer Experience Professional (CCXP), endorsed by the Customer Experience Professionals Association (CXPA).

5. **Network to learn.** I cannot stress the importance enough of networking! One of the reasons that I am so incredibly proud to form part of the CX community is that it is the most welcoming, supportive community I have ever encountered throughout my career. CX professionals are empaths at heart and, in my experience, are only too happy to support and share their experiences and expertise as you embark on your journey. Here I must mention my CX mentor, Ian Golding, who has been a constant source of support and inspiration. The CXPA themselves have also been a great source of support and guidance.

6. **Customer First.** It's essential to remember that customers are ultimately human beings, and much like each of us, no two are the same. We all come from different walks of life and have different past experiences. Continually work to view matters from your customer's perspective, not your own. For instance, I've done a lot of work on consciously considering our vulnerable customers and ensuring they are safeguarded and provided with maximum support while engaging with our organisation. These efforts include providing support materials to our colleagues to help navigate sensitive situations and accompanying dedicated training efforts, which ensure we place ourselves in our customers' shoes.

To summarise, regardless of where your organisation is on its CX journey, start by assessing which pieces of the puzzle you already possess. Then, work to align them and fill in any missing pieces. Remember that exceptional customer experiences don't just happen. Organisations delivering remarkable outcomes are the ones who consciously conceive what they want their desired Customer Experience to look like and implement strategies to deliver on their ambition.

Next, continually work alongside your people to ensure that everyone is pulling towards the organisation's aims in the same direction. However, words must translate into action. Simply talking about it isn't enough. Capture what the desired experience should look like and how you want your customers to feel after engaging with you in the form of your company's CX Strategy. Remember that the science of CX is centred around how customers feel about your organisation, as this ultimately drives their purchasing decisions.

As a word of advice, remember that Rome wasn't built in a day. It can be tempting to want to start tackling all areas with opportunities for improvement at once. However, this will not be viable and would surely be a plan to fail. Assess where the most significant impact will be felt with the limited resources available and work on implementing a framework in a logical order which makes sense for your organisation. Continually assess progress as you go and ensure that you are on the right path.

Whatever you decide to do, do something! Get started on raising the bar toward CX Excellence for your organisation. It's a long journey which takes a considerable amount of effort over a sustained period. However, it's incredibly rewarding to observe improvements made as a result of your work and to witness rising CSAT/NPS scores.

Remember that CX Excellence delivers business value for your organisation, providing a sustainable point of differentiation in the market that is arduous to replicate. While the competition can undercut you on pricing or introduce a new proposition to rival yours overnight, they cannot attempt to replicate your CX delivery without a significant, sustained effort over a substantial duration.

About Scott Lee Holloway

Scott Lee Holloway (CCXP) is an esteemed Customer Experience Professional spearheading the Voice of the Customer Unit at APS Bank in Malta. Scott ensures that the customer's voice resonates throughout the organisation, translating into an unparalleled customer experience.

Scott's commitment to excellence is underscored by over a decade of experience in the Financial Services sector, including working alongside industry titans such as Santander, HSBC, and Willis Towers Watson. While studying at The London Institute of Banking and Finance, Scott deepened his understanding of the Financial Services Industry, including Customer-Centric Practices and Complaints Management techniques.

A recognised authority in the field, Scott has delivered keynote addresses at prestigious events and CX forums. His expertise is further evident in his role as a judge at esteemed awards ceremonies, including the European Customer Experience Awards (EXCA), where he has been a part of the panel since its inaugural edition.

An unwavering dedication to professional development led Scott to become Malta's first-ever Certified Customer Experience Professional (CCXP) certified by the CXPA. Scott Lee Holloway is a dedicated CX professional and trailblazer shaping the future of customer-centric practices in the financial services industry.

LinkedIn *www.linkedin.com/in/scottleeholloway*

Website *www.scottleeholloway.com*

CX Strategy

CX Strategy That Works: Integral Approach

Olga Guseva

"Less than 1/3 of CX initiatives are successful" – says Bob Thompson in his research[1] and my heart stops for a second each time we start a new consulting project. The client invests valuable time, energy and devotion into something we truly believe in – and it still has a 70% failure rate. What is the reason behind this?

Twenty years of experience in marketing, management and customer experience tell me that successful companies are usually quite good at planning; we envision a bright future and create detailed plans. We are convinced these plans will work at the moment we create them, but... something happens afterwards. We get trapped by silos, urgent priorities, budget cuts, sales slowdowns, changing market conditions, and the plans don't come to fruition.

Having worked with companies in more than 20 different industries, I also see that in most of the cases teams successfully plan "tangible" aspects – what needs to be done, controlled, checked, created or manufactured.

Things get much harder when we start thinking, who will implement these tangible things and what can stop or impede these people. As a result, a "human side" of implementation often gets overlooked.

It simply does not filter through the lines of the table within a 5-year strategic plan.

After a while, we discover that some activities are falling behind or not being performing as they should. Frustration and pressure accumulate. The project manager is pushing to achieve deadlines, and it seems that everything is falling apart, the level of energy goes down and enthusiasm drains. Does this sound familiar?

What is missing? Why do lots of projects fail?

Including the "human side" into CX strategic planning is vital, there's no question about it, but how can we make sure we haven't forgotten something important?

To increase the "survival rate" of CX initiatives we at Integria rely on an integral approach, originally created by Ken Wilber, a philosopher that has nothing to do with Customer Experience. You may have heard about his books "A Brief History of Everything"[2] or "The Integral Vision"[3].

His theory goes well beyond business needs into the deepness of the human mind, but the essence of Wilber's approach brings valuable practical insights on how to increase the chances to successful implementation of CX strategy. In accordance with Wilber's approach, all events and entities in life have two major dimensions – the external, visible side, and an internal, invisible part. These two parts are deeply interconnected. Moreover, we can look at every person, company or state from an individualistic and from a collective point of view.

Still sounds a bit theoretical?

Let's have a look at the example.

If I am planning to go on a date, there will definitely be something that happens in my mind. I am excited, looking forward to meeting my fiancée. Of course, I am preparing for a date, so I choose a beautiful dress and wear attractive perfume. This is what happens on my individual level. Take it or hate it, but the two of us are already a system of two people, and for the period of several months that we date we are already used to meeting on Fridays and going to the theater or restaurant. This is visible, friends can see it in our social media posts. Between the two of us, there are also some unspoken rules: we don't discuss politics, we respect each other's time and we feel embarrassed when others are asking about the future of our relationship. Let's use Ken Wilber's approach and build a simple map that puts all this information about our date into a system:

	Internal	External
Individual	I am excited I look forward for a date	I choose dress I wear perfume
Collective	We prefer not to discuss politics We respect each other's time We feel embarassed when asked about our joint future	We meet on Fridays We go to the theater or restaurant

Figure 1: Ken Wilber's Integral approach applied to dating

We can apply this approach to any other event, project or system. Why is this important? If I understand what happens inside people's minds, I can predict their behavior. If I know what is happening between us, I can understand why I feel or behave in a specific manner. All 4 sections, or quadrants, as Wilber describes them, are closely interconnected and influence each other.

Integria have applied this approach to Customer Experience strategy and called it Strategic Map™.

Let's walk together through the whole process of creating the maps and building an integral CX strategy for your company.

STEP 1: Discover the reality

We can start by having a look at the quality of customer experience, discover the insights, find out what customers are feeling and thinking and how they are behaving. We can also look deeper inside the company and ask ourselves, how do we as a company interact with the customers. At the cultural level, how we as a company treat our customers (for example - as a gift, as a disturbance), do we really respect and value them or think that they are stupid and need to try again before calling us? Now, what does it look like from a systematic point of view? Which communication channels do we use, what messages do we send, how do we measure our performance with customers, how many calls do we accept per day. Finally, we can look one level deeper and ask ourselves, who builds this customer experience? How are our employees feeling? Because this will inevitably influence how they behave and interact with the customers.

Now we can put all these interdependencies visually in one map:

	Customer level	How customers feel and what do they think	What customers do, how do they behave
Visible	**Company level**	**Corporate culture:** unspoken rules of interaction with customers	**System:** how we as a company interact with the customers, what we measure
Invisible		Uspoken rules of interaction between employees	Which tools do we use, how good the current metrics are
	Employee level	How employees feel and what do they think	What employees do, how do they behave

Figure 2. Strategic Map™

The attentive reader can recognize the heritage of Ken Wilber's approach – there's a visible (right) and invisible (left) part, individual (at customer and employee level) and collective (at company level). We can even draw a horizontal line at the company level and divide the aspects of the corporate culture customers can see, hear and watch (for example, when employees are discussing other customers in the retail store), and the aspects that are hidden from the customers (when employees give certain customers nicknames, how employees are referring to the customer in the back office). In the same way, we can look at the company level and divide it into the part that customers can see and experience (how good the website is, how quickly call center agents are answering the calls, what happens when a customer raises a complaint) and processes that are hidden from the customers (for example, how do we process the data we have collected from the customers, how do we prioritize customer issues, how we delegate the responsibilities and maintain a website). As we base ourselves on the integral approach, we can be confident that we haven't missed something crucial – and experience shows that the most exciting discoveries are being made in the invisible part of the map.

We frequently use this approach in the format of strategic workshops – as a first step, participants collect what they already know about the customers and themselves. At this stage we can already discover some blind spots. This is a good indicator that we need additional information, maybe, a research is needed here. We usually ask participants to use different colors to mark positive and negative findings – this helps visualize the whole picture and discover the biggest drawbacks in customer experience and the internal processes that fuel it.

STEP 2: Envision the future

CX strategy is a road from A to B, from where we are now to where we want to arrive. After we have done the analysis of what happens with customer experience now and completed the AS IS map, we can move on and fill out the same map, thinking what kind of customer experience we as a company would like to create for our customers.

We can define how we want our customers to feel, what we want them to think and, as a consequence, do. Correspondingly, we can ask ourselves what kind of culture can support this experience and which processes and systems do we need to have in place in order to provide such an experience for the customers. Finally, we look deeper into the employee's minds, feelings and their actions. If the company is big and multi-layered, sometimes it makes sense to look at different employee groups - starting from top management, then middle management and line employees – again, it is always important to look at both visible (actions) and invisible (feelings and thoughts) parts.

STEP 3: Plan Your Journey

Strategic Map™ AS IS | **Strategic Map™ TO BE**

How customers feel and what do they think	What customers do, how they behave	How customers feel and what do they think	What customers do, how they behave
Corporate culture: unspoken rules of interaction with customers	**System:** How we as a company interact with the customers, and what we measure	**Corporate culture:** unspoken rules of interaction with customers	**System:** How we as a company interact with the customers, and what we measure
Unspoken rules of interaction between employees	Which tools do we use, how good the current metrics are	Unspoken rules of interaction between employees	Which tools do we use, how good the current metrics are
How employees feel and what they think	What employees do, how do they behave	How employees feel and what they think	What employees do, how do they behave

Figure 3. From AS IS towards TO BE

What comes next? We can use several approaches to build integral CX strategy out of these two maps:

- Look at the biggest customer problems we have listed. What irritates customers most? Where is the friction at maximal level? What can we do to fix it? By looking deeper at the left side of the table, we can discover the anxiety, the feeling of being ignored or reprimanded the customers are experiencing. Customer journey maps are an excellent source to fill out the first line of the Strategic Map™.

- Find the biggest gaps between AS IS and TO BE and see what stops us from being where we want to be. Are customers leaving to competitors, but we would like them to stay longer? Customers are posting negative reviews and this brings our reputation down? If you could make one or two key changes, where would you focus?

- Look at the interdependencies within each table and see what drives current customer behavior. It could be the website that is so slow and inconvenient that it forces the customers to call the contact center and ask for help. It could be the feeling that the company is looking for every opportunity to steal a penny from a customer's wallet driven by the sales oriented culture. Or it could be the impression that I am not important as a customer, driven by employee's belief that customers have no choice but to buy from us.

STEP 4: Make It Real

After we have discovered the key directions to follow to get from AS IS in the direction of TO BE, all we need to do is to bring these high-level activities down to earth with specific actions and set the deadlines and responsibilities for fulfilment.

The power of integral approach is in the confidence that by going through this process we have considered all vital aspects and did not leave a single stone unturned. We've set up the foundation to make sure our CX strategy will fall into the happy 30% of CX initiatives that get implemented successfully.

The approach is universal: it fits all industries, cultures and any size of the business. It is being successfully used throughout the world in psychology, teaching, early childhood education, public administration, medicine and many other areas of life where people interact with each other.

Try using it next time when you build your CX strategy and enjoy the discoveries you'll make along the way.

References

1. An Inconvenient Truth: 93% of Customer Experience Initiatives Are Failing…to Differentiate. Bob Thompson, February 7, 2018, Customer Think portal: *https://customerthink.com/ an-inconvenient-truth-93-of-customer-experience-initiatives- are-failing/*

2. A Brief History of Everything: Wilber, Ken, 1996

3. The Integral Vision: A Very Short Introduction to the Revolutionary Integral Approach to Life, God, the Universe, and Everything: Wilber, Ken, 2007

About Olga Guseva

Olga Guseva is a keynote speaker and global CX consultant voted Top 150 Global CX Thought Leader in 2020.

CCXP, CXPA Recognized trainer, member of the CXPA European Leadership Council and the member of the Board of Directors of Customer Institute.

Olga is a co-founder of Integria Ltd., CX consulting company that is using integral approach as a foundation to solve business challenges.

Below you'll find links to some additional materials that will help you apply the integral approach to CX strategy in your company:

Download a step by step guide how to create an integral CX strategy in your company:

Download a list of questions that will help you complete the AS IS and TO BE STRATEGIC MAPS™

Email: *olga@integria.ru*

LinkedIn: *https://www.linkedin.com/in/olgaguseva/*

Integria website: *integria.ru*

CX Strategy

How To Lead A Successful Customer Culture Transformation Using The Unconventional Bottom-To-The-Top Approach

Georges Essama

Leading people is one of the greatest challenges that exist. If you're a parent, you understand what I mean. I struggle every morning with my kids to prepare them for school on time. Trust me, I don't always succeed. Is that your case too?

If properly raising kids in this hyper-changing world is such an important challenge, imagine what it takes to infuse a customer-centric culture with hundreds or thousands of employees in a public organisation. How can this be done?

A universal answer to this question is surely not appropriate. Simply because every organisation is unique. What is usual is that you will have to go through an internal transformation. On that journey, you will need the right people to lead this initiative and a change model to implement. So what should those leaders do and which model should be used?

Surprisingly the model that fits your transformation challenge might not exist. You might be the one to create it. Organisations need good leaders to make the right changes. But they might not be those we usually think of (Executives or Senior leaders for example).

They could be operational managers or "SIMPLE" frontline agents. Anyone with the right mindset and determination to lead that transformation. It can be YOU. In fact, Your mission, should you choose to accept it, is to be the leader that your organisation needs to make the right changes and drive the positive transformation. Are you ready for that?

In this chapter I am going to share my experience of a successful and award-winning business case on leading a transformation, to build a customer-centric culture, in a complex environment, with unexpected people and using a non-conventional change management approach. How did we make it?

Let me start by setting the scene.

Imagine you work for a public company, with a complex and unstable organisational structure. A workplace with no clear career journey and a deficiency of collaboration. A catastrophic brand image and deplorable service at touchpoints. A place where the culture of bureaucracy dominates above the priority of offering good Customer and Employee Experience. Where personal and political matters have greater consideration than operational efficiency. In that company, you are not the CEO or a C-level manager. You are "JUST" a manager or frontline agent in an operational business unit. Far from the table where strategic decisions are taken, but close enough to daily operations, with direct impact on your organisational perimeter and customer perception. Can such companies still exist in this world?

This workplace is not an imagination but the reality of our company a few years ago. The change was more than an emergency. But how do you make a change if you're not in a highly distinctive role in the organisation? Is it possible from a "LIMITED" position to launch a "MOVEMENT" that will change customer's perception, engage operational teams and align an entire organisation to adopt best customer experience (CX) practices?

If you think it is impossible, then you are exactly at the

right place now. We will share five important lessons you can apply to be the change leader that all organisations look for. Someone using a simple approach and the S.I.M.P.L.E model to lead a bottom-to-the-top change management initiative. This model will provide you a step by step guide to navigate in troubled water and transform an organisation's culture to place customers at the heart of operations.

Lesson 1: Start From Where You Are

Are you a local branch manager? Functional leader or frontline customer care agent? No matter your role or position, start making the change in your direct organisational perimeter.

Many professionals think that they need to be appointed C-level managers to make the change they feel their organisation needs. Our experience is the opposite. From the operational perspective or your business perimeter, you can lead a transformation that will touch an entire organisation. What you have to do is start applying the best customer and people-centric practices where you are now.

We did the same and started in our organisational perimeter. An operational business unit in charge of a key region of the country. After making research, establishing a baseline, and identifying customer expectations, we defined a "LOCAL" CX transformation program for our sole business unit. The program focused on implementing best CX practices going from CX strategy, human-centred design thinking, voice of customer program, customer journey improvement …etc. This was a local initiative in alignment with corporate guidelines but implemented exclusively for our business unit and by local teams.

You can do the same. So don't wait any longer. Start from where you are and Start now.

Lesson 2: Inspire Yourself And Your Team

As a CX leader, your mindset, engagement and beliefs are major foundations to make a change. A famous brand says that "Impossible is nothing". In my home country, Cameroon, we usually say that "Impossible is not Cameroonian". These expressions reflect the fact that in every situation of "impossibilities" there are oceans of opportunities.

To be the right CX leader, your intrinsic beliefs and values have to be strong enough to challenge the status quo. Fuel yourself with leadership skills, abilities and intrinsic readiness to struggle and succeed. Forge in your mindset the idea that you can change your direct environment and your entire organisation to become more customer-centric.

In our case, a transversal and multifunctional task force of less than 10 passionate operational managers (0.25% of the workforce) launched the "LOCAL" CX transformation program of the business unit. It all started with the right leader's mindset and the belief that we could make it no matter the challenges we would go through. Don't wait for others to make the changes you have to.

Lesson 3. Mix The Right Ingredients

CX Transformation is like "cooking". Every cook needs the right ingredients, combination and action to produce a delicious meal. No organisation in the world is hard enough to change. You just need to know and use the right ingredients. In cooking TV programs, candidates all access the same components and materials but use them differently. The best cook is the one mixing ingredients the best way possible to generate the best result.

The logic with CX is similar. You need the right ingredients to build a successful customer-centric culture in any type of organisation. We will share with you three ingredients that will help you transform your organisational culture using the bottom-to-the-top approach.

- **Ingredient N°1: A dedicated operational leadership**
  The core of every company's soul is reflected in its operations. How are customers treated at touchpoints? How do frontline employees behave and what do they value? The role of the operational leadership is then critical. It is the last organisational layer to give the company a chance to do what is right for customers and employees. Make sure that you have the right people leading operations. People aligned with the best customer and people-centric values, passionate about what they do. If you don't have them, find them. And if you're concerned, be one of them.

- **Ingredient N°2: A proven Customer-centric operational approach**
  With the right operational people on board, define a clear operational plan. What do you intend to achieve from the operational perspective to make customer-centricity and change management a reality? This plan can be specific, innovative, and autonomous but always needs to connect with the corporate values of the organisation to be globally accepted by the corporate leadership.

- **Ingredient N°3: Exceptional relation skills to navigate across the organisation**
  If you want your change project to succeed, work close in hand with key organisational stakeholders. In companies with complex organisational structures, confusing decision-making processes, and complicated management approaches, "HIRE" on your side key stakeholders across the silos. People who are sincere and professional enough to appreciate the impact of your achievements. Close enough to the corporate leadership to testify the key role you play for the organisation. They exist in every workplace. Find them and connect with them.

Lesson 4: Prove with Clear Results

Actions speak louder than words and results speak for themselves. An operational plan that doesn't show clear results has a greater chance of failing the transformation. A Customer-centric approach with no impact on business indicators is a "NOISY EMPTY BARREL".

Six months after implementing our local CX transformation program, we increased the revenue of our business unit by 50%. Changing customer perception and improving indicators (CSAT from 64% to 86%, NPS from -20 to +25). The results of our program went above our business unit to impact the entire company. Our work became the internal benchmark to inspire our staff to achieve great results and implement best CX practices. The impact was clear and visible to all.

Lesson 5: Leverage Unconventional Approaches For Unconventional Situations

The CX leader is an open-minded visionary. In implementing a transformation the approach you use counts a lot. A common idea is supposing that an impulsion from the leadership to the base is the saint grail in making change happen. Another one is thinking that generic change models are suitable for every situation.

Exclusively using the top-to-bottom change approach doesn't always work. THERE ARE PLACES WHERE YOUR AUTHORITY IS NOT STRONG ENOUGH TO MAKE THE TRANSFORMATION HAPPEN. So you will need to use another approach. Driving Change from the bottom to the top is one of the alternatives.

This approach is about implementing best CX practices, starting from the operational layer of an organization, showing the proof of results, gradually getting consent and acceptance from the staff and progressively transforming an entire organization from the operational to the strategic Level.

Lesson 6: Excel In Making Your Achievements Visiblew

A good communication strategy to promote your achievements is gold. Add more visibility to the work you do inside and outside the organisation. Join global CX communities. Participate in international CX events, competitions and conversations.

As we shared our story with the global CX community, we participated in international competitions and gained more experience. We received various recognitions, which added more visibility, credibility and adoption to our initiative. You can do the same. Share what you do to improve your customer's and employee's lives. Everyone is waiting for that.

So, to summarise on the question of How to Lead a Successful Customer Culture Transformation using the bottom-to-the-top approach, the answer is S.I.M.P.L.E.

The Simple CX Transformation Model™

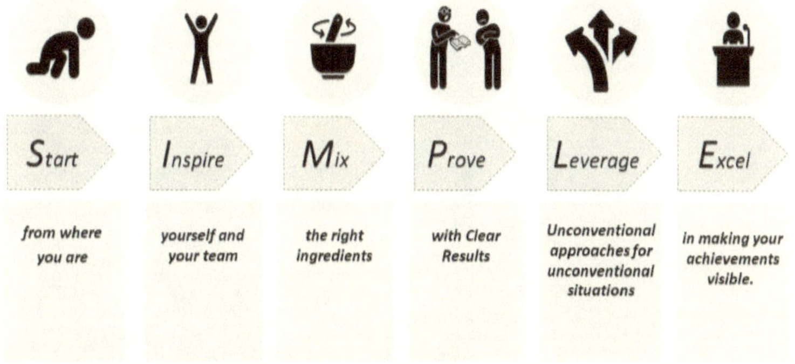

Sustainable transformations start with good foundations and great changes have small beginnings.

The lesson of our story is not just that putting customers and employees at the centre of your operations drives to Success. But the fact that no matter your level or position, you can change your direct environment and your entire organisation to become more customer-centric.

You can lead a change from wherever you are, "from Down to Up". This is good news for you, isn't it?

There will surely be hurdles to overcome. But always remember what a famous leader said: "YES WE CAN".

We also tell you today: "YES YOU CAN" and hopefully "YES YOU WILL".

About Georges Essama

Georges Essama is the first Certified Customer Experience Professional (CCXP) in Cameroon and Central Africa, with 12 years of experience in the telecommunication industry and public sector. He is actually Head of CX, Marketing and Communication at Cameroon Telecommunications.

He created TheService Foundation, a NGO dedicated to support CX transformation and advancement of the service culture and leadership for service.

He contributes globally to the CX knowledge as a judge for various CX competitions, Content contributor, Survey panel expert, Guest at various CX Podcasts and Keynote Speaker at CX events. Board member of the Customer Experience Professional Association (CXPA), 2023 Chair of CXPA Africa and multiple CX Awards winner (CX Leader of the Year Culture Award, CX Emerging Leader, CX Leader of the Year in Francophone Africa, Best CX Professional of the Year in Cameroon), he ambitioned to expand the CX knowledge to support the African community and transform African organizations.

Email *georges_essama@yahoo.fr*

Linkedin *https://www.linkedin.com/in/georgesessama/*

CX Strategy

Customer Experience Strategy

Gabriela Geeson

Introduction

Customer Experience has become a vital element to enable an organisation's success. It is now a critical differentiator. Organisations that prioritise giving their customers great experiences are the ones who are nurturing loyalty and are thriving in today's competitive environment. Loyal customers will enable organisations to stay in business. After all, without customers, organisations cannot operate.

In this chapter we are going to explore what it means to create a well-defined strategy, how to do it and some examples of some brands that are doing this effectively and as a result, are seeing a return on investment and a strong brand health. My hope is that you can be inspired to get started defining your own customer strategy to shape and manage your customers' experience positively.

Customer Experience Definition and Benefits

A Customer Experience Strategy is simply defining what experience you want your customers to have. It is creating a plan or a blueprint of the experience you want to offer your customers. It is a guide or a framework that will guide everyone in your organisation when making a decision that is going to have an impact on your customers. It is like when an architect designs the plans for the constructors to know what the end goal is.

Here are the main reasons it is important for an organisation to create a customer experience strategy:

Customer Loyalty and Advocacy

When customers are satisfied with your product or service and they feel valued, they are more likely to continue using your product or service, and they are going to become your biggest champions. For instance, I could not wait to tell my friends about a new restaurant I visited in town. Booking a table was very easy. I reported that I had a food allergy when I booked a table and they called me a couple of days before my visit to double check my allergies and confirm the details about my booking. They even shared the special allergies menu beforehand for me to take a look at. It saved me from the awkward conversation on the actual day. They understood it isn't a conversation you want to have when ordering your food and it can be done beforehand. In the customer experience world, it could be identified as one of those moments that matter in your experience as a user. The food was delicious and the service on the day was fantastic. I also loved the decoration of the restaurant and it was reasonably priced. Needless to say, my overall experience was great.

Revenue Growth

Satisfied customers naturally spend more. Organisations that provide great experiences are more likely to generate a higher revenue. In one of the tech businesses I worked for previously, we did a correlation analysis between Net Promoter Score (NPS) results collected over a three year period and how much each customer spent during that time. We found that Promoters used the service five times more in that period of time. We also found that they spent more, as the value of each transaction was higher.

We also found that if detractors would turn into promoters, it would generate almost £2.5 million pounds in additional revenue every year. The findings proved the hypothesis that happier customers are more likely to use the service or product. They are also happy to try any other product or services that might be offered by the same organisation, therefore increasing opportunities for cross sale.

According to a study conducted by the Qualtrics XM institute '94% of consumers who give a company a "very good" CX rating are likely to purchase more products or services from that company in the future. In comparison, only one in five of those who gave a company a "very poor" CX rating say the same'.

Competitive Advantage

Globalisation and access to a much wider range of products and services online, has meant consumers are spoiled for choice. There are many organisations out there, offering the same or very similar products and services. As a consequence, without a competitive advantage it is impossible to stand out from the crowd. Customer Experience can be a powerful and unique competitive advantage for your organisation, also resulting in sustainable growth. Let's think about booking a flight - two different airlines may fly to the same destination but one of them offers a better experience. I am more likely to use the airline that provides a better experience. That airline can even charge more as there are many users who will be happy to pay more in order to have a more pleasant experience.

Churn Reduction

A well executed customer strategy would help minimise customer churn. When customers find an organisation difficult to do business with and they are dissatisfied with the product or service received, they are more likely to look for another provider. Therefore a good customer experience can be the best tool to combat or prevent churn.

Reputation and Brand Health

Word of mouth is an important aspect of customer experience. Happy customers will want to recommend a product or service to others, sharing the good news, but on the flip side customers who have a negative experience, would want to discourage others from using it. Naturally, they won't want others to have the same negative experience. A customer experience strategy that is making customers happy is a great tool to ensure they are helping you to build that positive reputation. Online reviews have grown in popularity over the years. More than ever, users will look for reviews online before purchasing something. For one of the organisations I worked with before, I decided to surface our organisation reviews that were captured by an independent reviews platform on our website to help build that trust amongst our customers. It not only gave our customers the reassurance they needed to use our service for the first time but it also improved our conversion rate by 20%.

How to Develop a Customer Experience Strategy

Each one of us is in this profession to make the world better with one product or service experience at a time. We are making a difference by ensuring the organisations that we lead or work for, pay attention to the experience they are offering so that users can have the experience they deserve.

When it comes to developing and applying your strategy it is important to ensure that all the teams responsible for each stage of the customer journey are on board, as they will be delivering the strategy, but it is equally important to help each team to explore how that strategy applies to the role they play in delivering that experience.

Co-create your strategy

The strategies that are better adopted are those that are co-created instead of dictated. Facilitate the conversation and co-create a customer strategy with the different teams in your organisation. Workshop ideas with them and have a discussion about how you want the experience to be for your customers.

Customer Insight

Ensure your organisation has a good understanding of your customers' needs and expectations but it is important it is evidence based. Use all the insight available; your front line colleagues should have a lot of insight to share but if this isn't already available, you can conduct some customer research and simply ask your customers about it. There are different options to do that, such as: ethnography studies, surveys, online studies, etc. You can decide the best research method for your organisation or audience.

Experience goals

Define your customer experience goals and ensure your goals are aligned to the overall business strategy. For example, a train operator organisation might have a business strategy to expand their network to connect every city in Europe and the experience strategy would be that it is easy to do business, flexible and value for money.

Customer Journey Mapping

Map the main stages of the journey and key touch-points where your customers interact with your organisation. This will help your organisation to consider things from their customer perspective and potentially identify areas for improvement.

Customer Experience Measurements

We won't know if we achieve our experience goals if we are not measuring our customers' experience. It is important to have experience metrics in place. The most commonly used metrics are Net Promoter Score (NPS), Customer Satisfaction Score (CSAT) and Customer Effort Score (CES).

Initiatives Roadmap

This is the list of areas your organisation is going to focus on to improve your customers' experience. It can be a list of tactical and strategic priorities or short term vs long term priorities. To achieve the long term vision, you might want to break this down into milestones. Taking an agile approach to deliver customer experience initiatives is a great way to do it. The organisations that I've seen deliver more improvements to customer experiences are the ones who use agile methodologies. There is a long term goal to create a great experience but it isn't always possible to do everything at once. That's why breaking it down into smaller deliverables is a more efficient way to do it.

One Page Strategy

Summarise your customer experience strategy on one page. It should include your overall customer experience statement, your customer needs that should come from the research and insight available and your experience goals where you can articulate how you want the experience to be for your customers. Finally, some guidance or examples on what this means in practice.

Communicating your customer experience strategy

Everyone should not only be aware of the customer experience strategy but should understand how they can apply it to their jobs. We need to map our stakeholders and create a communications plan. Where possible, ensure the organisation's existing channels and forums are used. Each organisation is different so we need to consider the organisation structure, the different channels, forums, mediums, format and frequency of your communications.

Training and Coaching

A curriculum personalised to your organisation should be planned, where you can cover the different components of the strategy. A good starting point is to cover the basics, like what are experience metrics, how to use them, the list of experience priorities from your customers' perspective, the victories, progress and success stories.

Examples Of Business Strategies

It is heartwarming to see that there are many organisations out there that have earned a good reputation and recognition for their customer experience strategy. They think about their customer needs and put them at the centre of their business strategy.

Amazon

It is not only one of my favourite brands but their customer obsession has influenced positively the experience that other online retailers are offering. They have set expectations by offering next day deliveries, sleek returns and refunds processes, and a diversity of products that are very easy to order. I always remember visiting one of their offices in London for an event where it really struck me that they even have their customer strategy written on their walls for everyone to be reminded of. They also keep an empty seat in their meetings which represents their customers; it is a reminder about always considering what is best for their customers. They are now one of the biggest retailers in the world. I use a finance app that the other day highlighted the fact I spent almost £1,000 on Amazon in the last 12 months. I couldn't believe it but it makes sense as they make it so easy for me to get what I need from the comfort of my own home and have it with me the day after I order. They don't only simplify my life, but they do it for so many people and for that reason they are very successful.

Disney

They create very magical experiences but it does not happen by chance. They have taken the time to understand their customers, in order to make every touch point as magical as possible. But not only that, they are very consistent in the experience they deliver at each stage of their customers' journeys.

Let's think about their theme parks; they are truly amazing, not just for kids but for adults too. As their strategy is to create magical experiences, they even take care of things like creating parking systems so that customers find their vehicle easily after their visit. They know visitors are creating lovely memories and they want to take lots of pictures so they have free photographers to capture these magical moments too. I remember someone from the Disney Customer Experience team shared at a conference that they also have a strategy in place to ensure their bins get emptied before they are three quarters full. They understand that a bin full or some litter on the floor could ruin a magical visit or photo.

AirBnb

A very user-friendly platform that allows travellers to find very unique accommodation in different parts of the world, travellers can be connected with people who can host them in their own home or rent their whole place for the duration of their stay. It has really disrupted the hospitality industry as travellers now have more options and don't have to rely on a hotel for their stay. I just visited Paris a few days ago and I was able to stay at a lovely two bedroom apartment in the centre of Paris. It was a really beautiful place that helped immerse myself in the Parisian culture, more than if I'd stayed in a hotel. The host was very responsive so my overall experience was great. AirBnB is now also promoting activities you can do while you are on holiday, making it easier to do it, especially if it is a city or country you have not visited before.

Apple

Apple is a brand that not only creates very user-friendly products but they also think about the other touch-points that are important to give their customers a great end-to-end experience. Their stores are usually in nice buildings and their staff are trained to provide excellent support. They spend a lot of time thinking about their customer needs so that as a result, they can innovate and even anticipate their customers' needs.

Spotify

A live streaming music platform that is leveraging artificial intelligence (AI) to personalise their customers' experience. They are using technology to personalise the music their customers listen to. I listen to music in both English and Spanish and really love the very personalised playlist they create for me based on the music that I love. There is nothing better than listening to your favourite tunes. It is like when a friend invites you over to their home and they know you so well that it starts playing your favourite music.

Conclusion

We all can influence the experience we offer our customers but we cannot do it alone. It is a collective effort and what we can also do is facilitate the process of defining a customer experience strategy. Co-create a customer strategy with your colleagues. Highlight the benefits of having a customer experience strategy. Foster a culture of empowerment where your colleagues feel like they can use the customer strategy to make decisions and/or changes that are going to impact your customers' experience positively.

Make technology one of your allies to simplify and improve the experience of your customers. Ask your customers for feedback to understand their perception, needs and expectations but also to measure the experience they are having.

You can start small by utilising what you already have, such as customer contact records from your front line teams. You can then fill the gaps with surveys and other research initiatives. Close the loop and create a process that is continuously listening to customers, acting on their feedback. Shine your light - many organisations out there need people like you and I who can help them to understand their customers' needs so that they can design great experiences for them.

Many organisations still need to be very intentional about the experience they offer so that they can shift from giving random experiences to orchestrating a great experience for their customers.

About Gabriela Geeson MBA, CCXP, Customer Insight Lead at UCAS

Gabriela is a talented customer experience professional with over 15 years of experience helping organisations improve their customer experience. Gabriela has designed and implemented successful customer strategies across a number of industries - HealthCare, FinTech, EdTech amongst others. Gabriela is passionate about creating experiences that help organisations to build long term relationships with customers. Gabriela is the co-author of two best-selling books: Customer Experience 1 and 2.

She currently works for UCAS where she is implementing a Customer Experience Program for the different audiences they serve. Previously, Gabriela held senior customer experience roles at successful tech organisations such as: WorldRemit – one of the fastest growing tech companies in Europe. In her role, Gabriela set the vision for customers' experience in over 200 countries across the globe. Gabriela has also worked for Lloyds Pharmacy Online Doctor, one of the leading online doctor services in the UK where she set up and led a Customer Experience function and implemented innovative initiatives to improve Customer Experience and drive Customer Centricity.

Gabriela has served as a judge for prestigious customer experience awards, evaluating top brands on criteria like effectiveness, innovation and impact. This background provides unique insight into what sets apart the very best in CX.

With a track record of dramatically improving customer satisfaction and loyalty for organisations worldwide, Gabriela offers an insider's perspective on the future of CX and actionable advice for leadership teams ready to put the customer first.

Gabriela holds a MBA, is a Certified Customer Experience Professional and a Certified Scrum Master.

Linkedin: *www.linkedin.com/in/gabriela-geeson-a5089b2a/*

CX Strategy

Explore Emotional Depths: Dive into a Research-Driven CX Approach

Vaishali Dialani

Creating emotional experiences to build a stronger connection as a business is not rocket science; in fact, it's the very essence of what makes us, CX professionals 'architects of human experiences' excel in our roles. In a world driven by transactions and numerical metrics, infusing emotional harmonies into customer experiences is a deliberate, research-driven process. While managing emotional regulation at the frontline of the business is manageable, a more significant question for us to address is how can we evaluate, manage, and regulate customers' emotional experiences with our brand at a strategic level. This strategic level entails identifying, evaluating, analyzing, and implementing the emotions we want our customers to 'feel' at every touchpoint through research.

Understanding and identifying the emotions we aim to elicit in our users is a foundational step. While the intensity of emotions is perception-based and may vary from person to person, as a business, we can identify which emotions drive customer satisfaction and significantly impact our business value. To explore the realm of human emotions, you can employ the Junto Institute's wheel of emotions.

We are all aware of how emotions shape customer interactions;

a happy customer is more likely to continue purchasing a product, while an angry or upset customer may negatively impact our brand through the reach of social media. By prioritizing emotional intelligence in our CX strategies, we can build stronger, more resilient customer relationships that contribute to long-term business success.

So, where does research fit into this picture?

Research is the gateway to understanding and learning about something, especially in the realm of CX. The beauty of research in the CX domain lies in its ability to help us grasp our understanding by combining our soft skills, like active listening, empathy and two-way communication, with our technical research skills, such as data analysis and survey design.

Choosing the right research methodologies, which align with the business objectives, is pivotal. The array of methods available includes observation, surveys, interviews, ethnographic research, secondary research, field interviews, and more. The adoption of research-driven CX strategies brings significant advantages, elevating the emotional experiences we offer. These CX strategies translate into more engaged and satisfied customers who develop stronger loyalty to our brand. In simpler terms, by understanding and fine-tuning the emotions customers feel, we create better experiences, and this leads to happier customers who keep coming back for more, building a stronger connection with our brand and more revenue for the business.

For us to provide personalized experiences that connect customers with our brand and leave them feeling positive, we must co-create these experiences with them. Research can be a fun and engaging experience, allowing customers to feel like a part of the design process.

In this chapter, I will be sharing the CX research framework that has guided me over the years, and I hope it proves valuable for you too.

CX Research Framework

The 'CX Research' framework is about steering an intentional and thought-provoking approach to gathering the right insights and it is designed based on my extensive hands-on experience over the years. Having conducted over 100+ CX research projects across diverse industries ranging from fintech, healthcare, education, manufacturing and more I can vouch for its versatility in adapting to each project's unique requirement. The beauty of using the 'CX Research' framework is the *'practicality'* it offers to meet diverse needs.

Step One: Dive into Discovery

To comprehend your customers and business processes for directing the right CX research to shape your strategy and design, begin by immersing yourself in the discovery phase. Kickstart this phase by creating a 'current status document'. Initially, this document may consist of data fragments you gather about the business. Its structure can evolve as you accumulate more information.

As you engage in active conversations with key stakeholders and begin to learn more about the business, you'll uncover qualitative insights that go beyond raw data. These interactions provide a nuanced understanding of customers' emotional experiences, shedding light on their needs, pain points, and expectations.

A 'current status document' serves as the canvas to identify existing gaps in various input processes. It helps pinpoint areas where enhancements and optimizations are needed, all guided by the research findings. As you delve into the 'current status document' it becomes a map that acts as a foundation for identifying gaps, revealing what needs further understanding and clarity.

The primary sections for your exploration include:

- **Current State Document:** A compilation of your current knowledge and data.

- **List of questions:** A technique to identify discrepancies and shortcomings to gather insights.

By kick-starting this step, you'll have a clear path to decipher the areas that need more attention and fine-tuning, setting the stage for informed decision-making and a strategic research planning phase.

Step Two: Identifying Insights and Research Methodology

This step is a personal favourite, as it involves defining what you aim to discover and the methods you'll employ to gather this valuable data. Once you've compiled a list of questions, follow the next steps:

- **Categorization:** Categorize them based on business objectives or functionality. This categorization helps in understanding which stakeholders should be involved and the type of research methodologies that need to be considered, along with the emotional impact of these findings.

- **Insights type:** Consider the type of insights you seek. Do you need diagnostic insights to understand the current emotional landscape, or are prescriptive insights to guide future actions more relevant?

- **Research Methodology:** Choose the research methodology that best aligns with your goals. Select the approach that fits your needs, and keep in mind that a combination of methods might be ideal for a comprehensive understanding.

- **Prioritize:** As you delve into the research process, remember to prioritize questions based on your customers' needs, your business objectives, and their overall value. It's crucial to acknowledge the constraints of limited time, budget, and resources while ensuring that they do not hinder your experience design process.

Wise decision-making is essential when selecting research methods, ensuring that you focus on obtaining the most significant insights to drive your CX strategy forward. Remember, the ultimate goal is not to answer every question but to extract the most valuable insights that will help you curate and evaluate the right emotional experiences for business growth.

Pro tip: Maintain flexibility throughout the research process. While you may have a list of questions, don't feel confined by them. Adaptability is a cornerstone of effective research. Some questions may lose relevance as you progress, while new ones might emerge. Embrace the ability to adjust your research plan as needed to stay aligned with your evolving objectives.

Step Three: Scoping Out The Insights Gathered

Once you've gathered insights and identified learnings from different research methodologies, it's time to conduct a gap analysis to identify the scope of work. This includes tasks and actions that are both important and feasible from various technical and business process perspectives.

During this phase, document a research insights document and action points, including those related to improving or optimizing emotional elements in the customer journey. This document serves as a roadmap, summarizing the insights and potential actions that can be implemented from a business perspective to meet the organization's objective and create emotionally resonant customer experiences.

The insights gathered also play a crucial role in shaping the emotional elements you want to instil in your customers. This consideration is essential when designing and creating customer journeys, which are part of the next phase.

Step Four: Injecting Insights into Action

This step marks the heart of your CX strategy. Now that you've understood how research leads to valuable insights and have scoped out the work, you can put your plans into action.

Begin by identifying alignment, ensuring effective communication, and gaining a deep understanding of the optimal way to create customer journeys and touchpoints. All of these actions should be guided by the approvals you've obtained from the organization and the buy-in from all stakeholders, ensuring the successful implementation of the strategy.

These insights are not the end but the beginning of your CX journey, and this is where the emotional elements come to life. They form the foundation of a roadmap that influences behaviours and activities. Additionally, consider the KPIs you want to introduce into your CX strategy. It's crucial to align your approach not just with the available time and budget but also with the resources at your disposal. Below is a glimpse of a few insights I gleaned from my recent projects across diverse industries to show how insights shape the business scope of work and enhance CX journeys.

Customer Journey	Touchpoint insights learnt	Actions	KPIs
Onboarding app users for the first time on a financial mobile app	1. No option to Reset the Password	1. Implement a secure verification process for password resets	1. Password Reset Success Rate

	(continued)	(continued)	(continued)
	2. Frustration and confusion due to a complicated navigation 3. Lack of clarity on documents Required leading to delay in completion 4. Users might feel anxious about the onboarding progress	2. Simplify the app's navigation structure 3. Clearly outline the necessary documents and provide template visual examples 4. Include a progress tracker to provide a sense of control and reduces uncertainty	2. Results from usability testing or measuring the most complicated touchpoint 3. Average time taken to complete the document process 4. Onboarding Completion Rate
Identifying helpful product manuals and resources on the manufacturer's website	1. Lack of clarity on the need for detail-oriented resources making users feel over-whelmed 2. Poor navigation and page scrolling as users struggle to find the wresources required for product installation	1. Implement self-help tool tips to educate users on the need for particular resources in their purchasing journey, alleviating fee lings of anxiety *> Inject self-help guides where required, delivering a sense of control* 2. Better Placement of Resources in the Main Menu *> Improve search functionality to expedite users' resource finding, making them feel more confident and less frustrated.*	1. Resource Accessibility Rate 2. User Satisfaction Score with Resource Discovery

The above examples are from diverse industries, yet the common thread between them is the CX approach injected to enhance better experiences. With the mobile app project, we observed a 40% increase in the success rate of password updates as users logged in and updated the app within first three months. Simplifying the app's navigation resulted in users completing the onboarding process in 85 seconds, compared to the previous 150 seconds.

We utilized heatmap tools to evaluate users' activity on the app and noticed that users were clicking on the tooltip designed to provide clarity on document types for visual images. Additionally, during ethnographic research post-implementation to experience and gather firsthand feedback, we were delighted to hear expressions like 'this is so easy now' as one of the most common reviews. Witnessing the elevated happiness on users' faces as they onboarded themselves was truly heartwarming and a clear CX strategy win.

On the other hand, with the manufacturing site project, our CX research results provided an interesting overview. From gathering requirements through interviews, usability testing to seeking help from SEO tools and experts, we were able to make more informed, data-driven decisions to design a better customer experience. The suggestions provided to solve people's pain points have already won the hearts of diverse stakeholders involved in the process. We can't wait for the site to go live very soon and monitor the positive user behavior!

Summary

Research is a pathway to learning, and emotions are the essence of what people feel. To craft an exceptional CX strategy, the journey begins by comprehending how individuals feel in their current experiences and envisioning the emotions you wish to evoke once you've tailored the right experiences for them. Recognizing this clear gap in creating the perfect emotional triggers will sharpen your intuition as a CX professional, allowing you to design journeys that foster business growth and leave lasting impressions.

So, if there were only three takeaways that I would like you to ponder, they would be:

- The research process can be messy and unclear at first, so stay resilient and uncover the real treasure of insights.

- Document everything you learn; it's easier to connect the dots.

- Keep a fair balance of emotional and analytical processes to do justice to the process.

Remember, as a dedicated CX professional striving to shape a holistic experience, it's imperative to apply a comprehensive research and experience design approach. So, find enjoyment in the process, have fun, and get into your research groove now to dive into the emotions that can transform your CX landscape!

About Vaishali Dialani

Vaishali Dialani is a multi-award winning CX professional in the Middle East. Recognized as a CXPA Emerging leader, CX Leader of The Year 2023 Finalist, and ranked among the top 11 CXMStars worldwide, she firmly believes in the power of knowledge sharing to foster growth and awareness within the CX community.

With over 8 years of experience as a data-savvy experience designer, research specialist, and strategic change-maker, she passionately advocates for integrating emotions and efficiency through customer experience research, product insights, and communications.

As a Senior CX Strategist at Konabos, a leading digital transformation consulting firm, she helps businesses understand their customers, define strategies, design customer journey maps, and foster cross-collaborative cultures. Her unique blend of creative and analytical perspectives drives CX innovation, ensuring the delivery of exceptional customer experiences.

Vaishali's commitment to knowledge sharing extends to podcasts, blogs, guest lectures, speaking engagements, and training programs. She also conducts leadership training workshops for low-literacy level professionals, making a positive impact through collaborative efforts across diverse spheres.

LinkedIn: *https://www.LinkedIn.com/in/vaishalidialani*

CX Strategy

WHW: The Model Of Conscious Leadership. Your Investment Of A Lifetime

Natalia Kim

What separates successful CX projects from unsuccessful ones? What is the most effective CX tool? Success is often associated with greater alignment with goals, greater results in less time, or outstanding performance.

In recent years, I've seen a significant increase in business demand for customer experience. Business tasks are becoming more ambitious for CX teams, and the complexity of tasks is increasing. Despite this, many CX professionals are still relying heavily on tools, looking for innovative approaches, new tools and success stories from other companies, while leadership is becoming a critical success factor.

Leadership is not just for those who hold the title of CCO. Think of yourself as a leader in your own life and in all the projects you undertake. My 15 years in customer experience management and 10 years in leadership development show a direct correlation between leadership development and customer experience success.

In customer experience management, as in any form of management, the word "management" is the key, and that's where I'd like to focus our attention. Let's remember, what is management? It's getting from A to B.

Who is the strongest CX leader and manager, able to earn the trust of the CEO and peers, authority and budgets? Surely it's the one who can lead the company and the team from point A to point B quickly, efficiently and happily, planning the time and actions that will get them there.

But what determines whether results are achieved or not? Not all actions are equally important. Two leaders may use the same tool, but achieve different results in the same time frame.

This chapter is dedicated to the nuances of leadership development. It will be particularly relevant to you if you find that what you're doing isn't as effective as it used to be, if you're looking for a new way forward, if you feel you've reached a ceiling in your professional development, or if developing leadership skills is important to you.

Let's discover what enables someone to achieve new results, engage, inspire and lead others.

WHW: the model of conscious leadership

We all know from early childhood that if we want to make a difference in the outside world, we need to take actions. Let's take a look at the different levels of influence and the results they can bring.

Level 1. WHAT: The level of tools

At the very first level of changes, the impact and results are small.

At this level we answer the question "WHAT"? What do I need to do to get what I want? Here we explore new tools, approaches and gain knowledge to understand WHAT needs to be done.

It may seem enough: we act and get results. We do it again and we get results again.

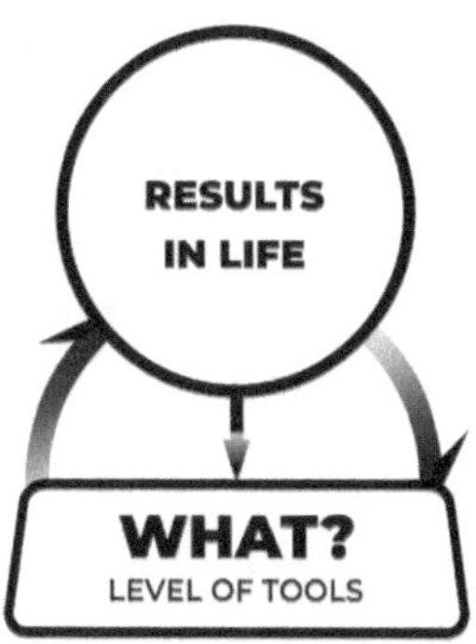

You may have heard the famous line attributed to Albert Einstein: "Insanity is doing the same thing over and over again and expecting different results." When we do the same thing, we get the same results.

If we are satisfied with these results, we can remain complacent and don't change anything, but external changes can intervene and we no longer even get the previous results. And what if we need a new result?

When old tools and actions no longer work, it often seems that we need to find a new tool, master it quickly, apply it and get the desired effect. This could be a solution, but it still works on the same level of tools, within a small circle of influence and results, so we keep going round in circles.

Culture also encourages us to stay within this small circle. As a result, a significant proportion of humanity and companies could spend their entire lives making small changes and achieving small results. Is there a way to get bigger results?

Level 2. HOW: The Level Of Mastery

Some people, due to their mindset, upbringing and level of thinking, are able to reach the second level. This is the level of skills - the "HOW" level, a medium circle of influence and results.

Here the focus is not only on WHAT to do, but also on HOW to do it. At this level we refine our skills in using the tool.

On reflection we can think of examples of such people or even recognize ourselves here. We often refer to them as true masters. It takes time to reach this level. However, the results obtained are no longer directly proportional to the actions, as they were at the tool level, but now show the effect of the Pareto Principle - 20% of the effort produces 80% of the results.

This is an intermediate circle of influence and results. The actions at these two levels can be the same, as can the time, but the results are different.

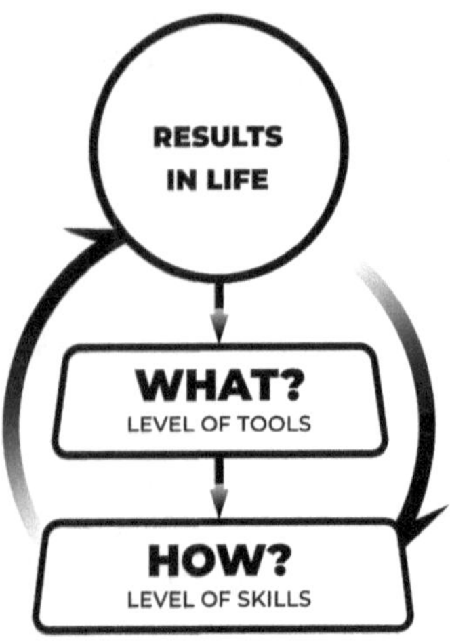

The level of proficiency is not the same as "years in the profession". It is crucial to understand that the level of skill is not just the time spent, but HOW that time has been spent. I could be busy as a bee for 10 years and my skills in using the tool will improve, but I won't automatically become a master.

What makes a master? It's more an act of will, a conscious path of self-improvement. It's a focus on how I do things, what I can improve, a willingness to listen to feedback from colleagues, deep personal reflection rather than borrowing someone else's ready-made theories, even if they come from a guru in the profession.

The mastery level is a journey into depth. It's about diving deeper into the methodology or tool each time. Fewer people and companies are moving to this level, especially now. You might ask why, if the results are so impressive? There are many reasons, but modern culture is definitely one of them. Most people are looking for speed, ease, simplicity and joy. The path to mastery is not quick, it takes time. It's not easy and it takes effort. And it's not always about joy and positive emotions. To improve, you have to see your imperfections, and that is not always pleasant.

Level 3. WHO: The Level Of Personality

Not everyone is ready to reach the second level, but only a select few are ready to move on to the third level. In any action we can always see WHAT (the level of tools) a person is doing and HOW (the level of mastery) he/she is doing it. And there's also WHO is doing it.

The level of personality - the "WHO" level - is a large circle of influence and results. The size and strength of a personality always directly influences actions and results, taking them to a new dimension.

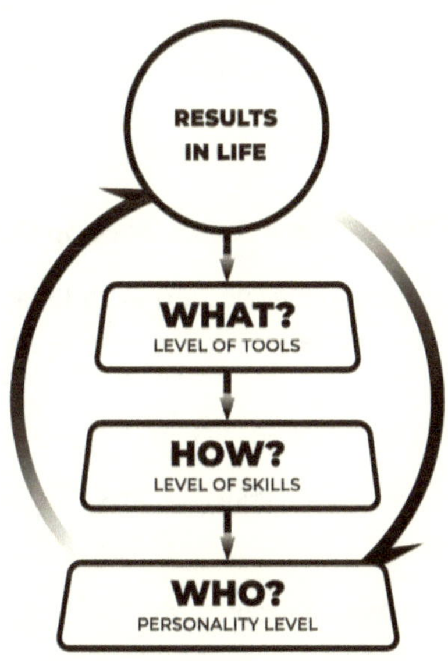

Can you think of an outstanding result achieved by a team or a company? Think about the leaders behind it. Ask yourself: "If I learned what they did (like Steve Jobs or Cristiano Ronaldo), and even understood how they did it, would I achieve the same results?" Obviously the answer is no. It's not enough.

So what exactly creates such results?

When we talk about leadership and management, we realise that it's not just about actions or management skills - it's the scale and strength of personality that affects teams and people, that engages, unites and moves the team forward.

I was once talking to the CEO of a large international company. I asked: "Why didn't you approve the investment in a CX project, even though the plan was interesting?" He replied: "It's not about the plan, it was excellent. The figures are perfect, as are the calculations and arguments. But they are not the most important thing. I don't invest in business plans or calculations. I invest in people. Either I see the personality that can implement all these plans, or I don't. It's about the strength of the personality. I look for their ability to make it happen."

If we listen to ourselves, we understand what this is about. It is not about being famous or having a strong personal brand. The size and strength of the personality is not equal to these external factors.

How Do These Three Levels Develop Over Time?

First we invest time in developing each level, and then these levels start working for us.

- Level 1. WHAT - Actions = Results.

- Level 2. HOW - the Pareto Principle: 20% of actions produce 80% of results.

- Level 3. WHO - a quantum effect, synergy. 1+1 equals more than 2.

As soon as one element of WHO changes, it changes all the above levels - the tools themselves and the mastery of their use are instantly and completely changed. The level of WHO works in opposite direction as well. When the abilities at the personality level are low, the development of higher levels is also limited. You can water the sand or fertilize the soil, and the results will be quite different.

The good news is that you don't need extra time to develop your personality, or to wait until you have mastered the previous two levels. These are parallel paths - the external path of skill development and the internal path of personality development.

It doesn't matter where you are at the moment - whether you're just starting out in your career and learning to use the tools, or have been a master in your field for a long time. Everyone can start their internal development journey right now.

The Path Of Personality Development

You hold this book in your hands in different parts of the planet and there's no universal way. I can only guide your thoughts and your search by sharing what I use for myself and my clients to make faster progress on the inner path of personality development.

In 15 years of internal work I have tried many different methods and approaches. Some proved ineffective, some very slow, while others remain with me to this day.

- **Meditation and clarity of thought** - observing yourself in three centres (emotions, mind, body)

- **Emotional Maturity** - practices for managing emotional states, including neuro-energetic techniques

- **Healthy Body** - Body techniques - through movement, meditation in motion, working on harmonising the flow of energy in the body.

- **Development of meta-skills** – awareness, integral thinking, mindfulness, behavioral flexibility and others.

I found all this at the Samadeva Free University in France. I know that representatives of the University are working all over the world, from Brazil to China.

You'll need like-minded people and guides/coaches/psychologists to help you on your journey. How do you choose them? Most importantly, look at WHO is in front of you, observe how this professional lives. They cannot be a wheelbarrow without a wheel. How emotionally mature are they, what kind of relationships do they build with different people, how do they react to conflict situations, how do they deal with difficulties, how do they manage themselves and to what extent are they good managers of their own life? Is there a serenity, a love and a joy in them?

Many people are now looking for the most efficient way to make the most of their lives in all their beauty. The best investment you can make is to invest in yourself. You are the most important tool in this life.

Wishing you a beautiful journey!

About Natalia Kim

Natalia Kim is the CEO of Integria LCC, the founder of CX University, the President of Russian Association of Customer Experience Professionals.

She is the founder and one of the key lecturers at the "Chief Customer Officer", a 9-month CX educational program for CX professionals with international certification. She has been involved in customer experience management since 2011.

Natalia's second area of expertise is the development of people and organizations with eight diplomas from different schools and areas of psychology since 2010. Executive coach, psychologist, author of personal development for leaders and teams. Member of the Professional Psychotherapeutic League.

Through her knowledge and deep understanding of human psychology, Natalia makes a significant contribution to the science of CX, enriching it with the scientific knowledge of psychology and neurophysiology. This allows CX experts to manage customer experience more consciously, improve existing CX tools and create new models.

Email *Natalia@integria.ru*

Website *www.integria.ru*

Organisation Structure and Culture

Organisation Structure and Culture

How Service Management complements CX by reinforcing Closed Loop with Continual Service Improvement

Steve Belgraver

Successful companies manage their Customer Experience intentionally. Companies that listen to their customers and use those insights to improve the way they work for a better customer experience have a competitive advantage over those that don't. In the world of CX this process is often called Close the Loop or Closed Loop for short. The potential value of having a process in place that continually produces better results is underscored by the fact this appears in many guises. CX's Closed Loop is complemented by a plethora of improvement management methodologies, frameworks and approaches of which several are more equal than others to misquote Orwell.

In this chapter, I will share with you my experience of working with a mindset of Continual Service Improvement (CSI) as a best practice distilled from the world of ITSM (Information Technology Service Management) which resonates particularly strongly with Closed Loop and helps produce a more robust way to improve the customer experience.

So where did the concept of Service Management come from? Along with agriculture and industry the third pillar of the modern economy is services. The Service Economy arose in the 20th century with the start of the Digital Age roughly half a century ago helped accelerate the rise of Service Management as a discipline to the point today where it is a fundamental pillar to the future for most organizations. These days there are numerous ways in which information technology is crucial to many organizations from business to education to health to finance and more. As organizations learned to harness the potential of IT and developed best practices, the ITIL (Information Technology Infrastructure Library) framework began to take shape during the 1980's in the UK. The principle of Continual Service Improvement entered the ITIL canon in V3 and continues in its current form as ITIL4 as part of the Service Value System.

Customer Experience (CX) actually started before the Digital Age going back to the development of market research and consumer theories before WW2. The advent of call centres followed by the emergence of enterprise feedback management systems heralded the age of CX. Although there isn't a single CX framework most if not all subscribe to the fundamental importance of listening and acting on customer feedback, also known as Closing the Loop.

The Net Promoter Score (NPS) developed in 2003 by management consultant Fred Reichheld from Bain & Company as a simple way to measure the customer loyalty of an organization helped raise the profile of Closed Loop. Around the same time Bruce Temkin, who some consider the Godfather of the Customer Experience, established Forrester's practice focusing on enterprise-wide customer experience. Although since then other management consultancies have contributed to the development of the CX discipline, Forrester arguably remains the one of the most influential research and advisory firms in the world customer experience.

So let's see how ITIL and Forrester define two key concepts.

- ITIL[1] defines service management as a set of specialized organizational capabilities for enabling value for customers in the form of services

- Forrester[2] defines customer experience as how customers perceive their interactions with your company.

I see Service Management and CX as essentially two sides of the same coin! The former provides the service experience while the latter experiences the service. And each discipline has its own ways to improve the way it realizes improvements.

The CSI[3] model guides support improvement initiatives and increases the likelihood that improvement initiatives will be successful. It puts a strong focus on customer value and ensures that improvement efforts can be linked back to the organization's vision.

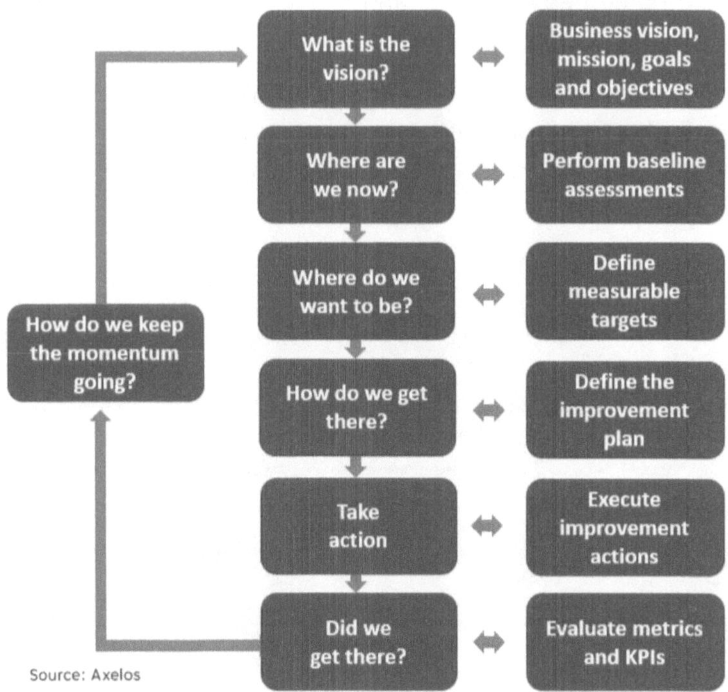

Source: Axelos

The model supports an iterative approach to improvement, dividing work into manageable pieces with separate goals that can be achieved incrementally. It aims to continually improve the effectiveness and efficiency of (IT) processes and services. Although the CSI model consists of a seven-step process, we need to remember this best practice remains a guide which means it is not prescriptive but rather one that is adopted and adapted by organizations based on their own situation and needs.

Unlike CSI, Customer Experience does not have a single universally agreed methodology which has led to many different Closed Loop frameworks around. That said, most organizations that employ a Closed Loop process agree on the basic principles of having a systematic cycle of making significant changes based on customer feedback. The aim is to improve business performance across the customer journey (i.e. all of the interactions customers have with an organization that shape their perceptions of and feelings towards the business) for a better customer experience.

But what does Closed Loop look like then? Below two examples, one from Bain who came up with the popular NPS system and the other from Medallia, a Gartner Quadrant and Forrester Wave Leader.

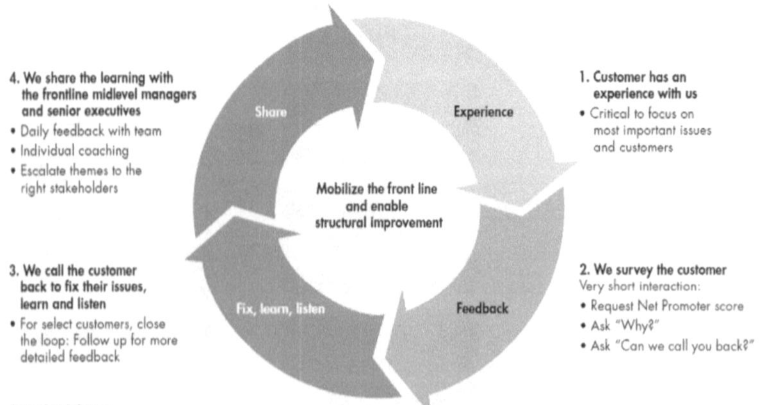

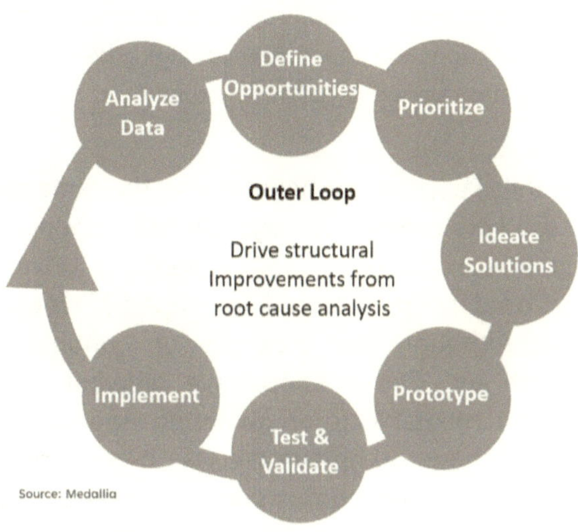

Despite Closed Loops differing in detail most if not all follow a number of common steps that involve collecting feedback, analysing it to come up with improvements, implementing those improvements and checking to see if and how these lead to a better customer experience. It's worth noting like CSI this is an iterative and continual process. Common metrics used in Closed Loop is the aforementioned Net Promoter Score (NPS) along with Customer Satisfaction (CSAT) and Customer Effort Score (CES) to name a few with scores often on a 10 point or Likert (5 point) scale.

Important similarities between CSI and Closed Loop are:

- Both are based on the concept of continual improvement and use methods from quality management to learn from past successes and failures.

- Both involve collecting feedback from customers or stakeholders, analysing it, identifying areas for improvement, implementing changes, and measuring the impact of those changes.

- Both aim to increase customer satisfaction, loyalty, and retention by delivering value and meeting or exceeding expectations.

- Both require coordination and collaboration among different business functions and teams by encouraging better alignment and integration along the customer journey.

Because these approaches help achieve the same objectives they are also very complementary. Whereas Continual Service Improvement can be considered a numbers driven logical exercise, Closed Loop is rooted in empathy, emotions and experience. Although the concepts of Continual Service Improvement and Closed Loop have different roots, they share the fundamental focus on gathering input and feedback for insights on how to improve the way organizations create experiences and deliver products and services to customers. Both share the concept of learning from past successes and failures to identify and implement changes to increase customer satisfaction. With its operational IT background CSI potentially adds some helpful rigor to Closed Loop which more often than not is a marketing led activity. In fact, these different approaches each with their own heritage but shared aims make them uniquely complementary and arguably work best when combined. By combining similar key concepts from both methodologies we end up with a simple iterative four-step process that improves the quality of products and services for continually improving customer experience.

1. IDENTIFY
CTL - collect client feedback
CSI - gather the data, identify root causes

3. IMPLEMENT
CTL - fix the problems
CSI - execute improvement actions

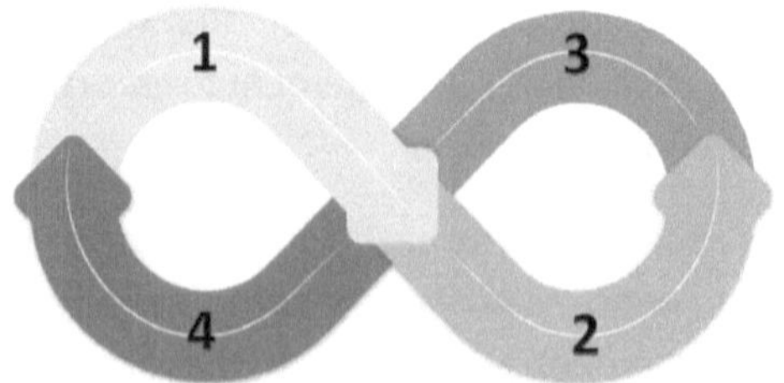

4. CONFIRM
CTL - follow up, close the loop
CSI - evaluate the results

2. ANALYZE
CTL - understand the pain points, develop recommendations
CSI - decide on improvement opportunities, define success measures

Finally, it's worth noting that there also are some differences between CSI and Closed Loop such as:

- CSI takes an inside-out approach by focussing on improving IT processes and services within an organization, while Closed Loop takes an outside-in perspective by starting with the customer experiences to improve the multiple touchpoints across the customer journey

- CSI is part of a single international framework (ITIL) based on industry best practice that uses structured methods to gather and analyse data and implement improvements, while CX is a newer field with varying approaches to Closed Loop by using more flexible methods to collect and act on feedback, and follow up with customers.

Summary

To summarize, there are a number of improvement methodologies and frameworks businesses use to make measurable improvements in their processes for a better customer experience. The CSI process from Service Management is a particularly strong contender when casting about for a way to continually improve the service experience that resonates well with CX. CSI and Closed Loop are approaches that share important similarities in their objectives, processes, and benefits of continual improvement. Although they also have some differences in their scope, methods, and requirements, both approaches can help organizations achieve better outcomes for their customers and stakeholders. Arguably, despite their differing provenances but shared aims, these frameworks are so complementary in fact that an integrated version of both should be used by any organization seeking to improve the way they work for a better customer experience.

References

1. https://purplegriffon.com/downloads/resources/itil4-foundation-glossary-january-2019.pdf

2. https://www.forrester.com/blogs/definition-of-customer-experience/

3. https://www.axelos.com/resource-hub/white-paper/itil-guiding-principles-for-continual-improvement

About Steve Belgraver

Steve is a Service Management professional with 15+ years experience in the world of B2B enterprise Telecoms and System Integrators.

After earning an MBA his passion for improving the client experience led him to discover the field of Customer Experience. Enriched with a multicultural background by having worked and lived on three continents, having completed degrees at several universities and bolstered with several CX and Service Management certifications makes him an authority on where the worlds of CX and Service Management meet.

Having managed multinational client accounts to running teams to establishing new business functions Steve has a deep understanding of how different business functions spanning the corporate journey influence the customer experience. By advocating the CX perspective he continually strives to collaboratively ensure the business executes on their commitments to meet client expectations.

Email *stevebelgraver@outlook.com*

Linkedin *https://www.linkedin.com/in/stevebelgraver/*

Twitter (X) *https://twitter.com/SteveBelgraver*

Organization Structure and Culture

The Financial Management of Experience

Sebastien Munar

Many companies may rush to see the bottom-line benefits of a customer-centric strategy: happier customers, higher loyalty, lower cost of service, and more engaged employees. Whilst these are tangible benefits, to me, it shows that they often don't clearly understand the value of a superior customer experience and exactly how it will create value.

Generally, companies undertake disruptive initiatives and projects to win over customers; but they don't quantify the economic results of differences in customer experiences (As Is vs. To Be), so their efforts end up having unclear short-term results. Without a quantifiable link to business value and a solid argument aligned to financial results, these efforts often cannot show gains and do not build momentum among executives; thus, they stall in early stages and do not achieve the potential long-term benefits that may have been possible.

The traditional approach has always been to calculate the impact of CX through Return on Investment (ROI), which is only a point-in-time look at an initiative and does not consider a holistic view of value generation across the company. In this chapter I will share with you my thoughts on how to the long term benefits of delivering a superior customer experience and hopefully inspire you all to take a longer term view.

From Customer Economics 1.0 to Customer Economics 2.0

I believe that customer experience must mature to the stage of a fully demonstrable and manageable business discipline at the financial level. For that, it is necessary to prove methodologically how the generation of a better management of our customers can have an impact on the economic results of companies. Also, we should be clear the adverse economic effect of a poor customer experience.

In fact, to achieve this in a sustainable and repeatable way over time, it is essential to have a framework that allows us to understand all the dimensions of what I call CX Economics 2.0: "The Financial Management of Experience".

I use those words on purpose; in fact, in my opinion customer experience has been developed for a long time in a very superficial way at the level of business impact, under practical ROI methods but which simplified many assumptions, and therefore reduced adoption in organizations. That is why I am convinced of the need to bring Finance, through more advanced tools, closer to the experience discipline by solidifying the professional management of client strategy. Having worked in both finance and customer experience motivated me to unite both paths, which for many years were dissociated, but are two sides of the same coin. We cannot talk about customer strategy without finance, and vice versa. This is the reason why I created the XQUEMA model.

The Financial Management of the Experience
through XQUEMA

The XQUEMA model (eXperience's QUality Economics MAnagement) is the result of my experience in different sectors, projects, markets and strategically mixing several disciplines. For several years I have seen firsthand that many highly experienced CX professionals have difficulty speaking the language of finance and comfortably explaining how their strategies make a real impact. And on the other hand, many financiers simply don't understand about the client experience, see the discipline as superfluous, and have a hard time "trusting" their peers. This challenge was the initial spark to convince me to go ahead with XQUEMA. This model consists of six dimensions that allow to condense what is required for a correct financial management of the experience:

1. **Financial Team Involvement:** Involvement of the financial team in identifying and collaborating in the analysis of financial aspects of the customer experience.

2. **CX Economics Vision:** Integration, awareness and deepening of the CX Economic vision (quantitative-financial impact mindset) in the culture and strategy of the company.

3. **Segmentation and Metrics Management:** Generation of the segmentations required to carry out Economics, and the measurement and management of CX and business metrics.

4. **Analytical, Statistical and Behavioral Tools:** Use of tools and techniques to collect, analyze and understand CX data and link it to financial impact.

5. **ROI Impact & Project Scaling:** Calculation of CX ROI, identifying the economic value per project and its scalability and replicability.

6. **Financial Management Evaluation & Governance:** Steering CX for impact on financial results and guiding strategic decisions and resource allocation.

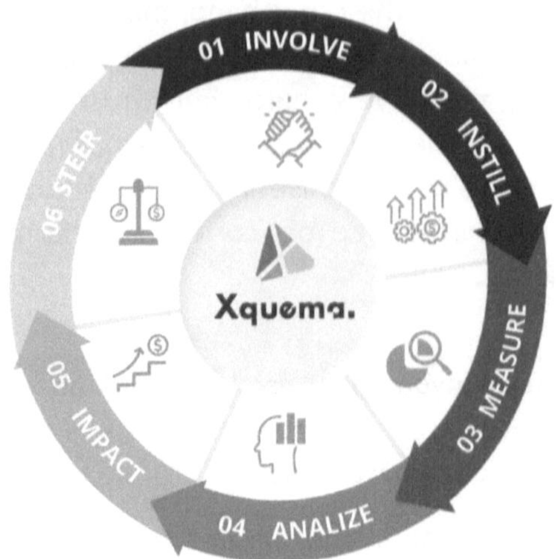

FINANCIAL TEAM INVOLVEMENT

Involves the finance team in identifying and collaborating on the analysis of financial aspects of the customer experience.

01

CX ECONOMICS VISION

Assesses the integration of the CX Economic vision into the company's culture and strategy.

02

SEGMENTATION AND METRICS MANAGEMENT

Examines the segmentation required to perform CX Economics, and how CX and business metrics are measured and managed.

03

STATISTICAL, ANALYTICAL, AND BEHAVIORAL TOOLS

Reviews the use of tools and techniques for collecting, analyzing and understanding CX data and linking it to financial impact.

04

ROI IMPACT & PROJECT SCALING

Calculates the ROI of the CX, identifying the economic value per project and its scalability and replicability.

05

FINANCIAL MANAGEMENT EVALUATION & GOVERNANCE

Identifies how CX impacts financial results and guides strategic decisions and resource allocation.

06

CX Economics Model: XQUEMA

The generation of a "Financial Management of Experience" model goes beyond the numerical part, but also has components as relevant as integrating a common economic vision, a governance that supports the incorporation of new quantitative practices, and above all how we enhance the linkage with increasingly advanced techniques. This is a long road, but it is important to start to ensure the sustainability of any transformation of experience.

Dimension 1: Financial Team Involvement

Assesses the extent to which the company's finance team is actively involved in identifying, measuring, and analyzing the financial aspects related to the customer experience. Thus, the level of involvement and collaboration of the finance team with CX teams should be measured enabling informed decision making and a more holistic view of the profitability and effectiveness of CX initiatives.

Something I have consistently seen in companies that master this dimension is that they scrupulously define goals and experience objectives related to the company's financial results, which helps ensure that CX initiatives meet profitability, risk, and strategic impact criteria to maximize their likelihood of success.

Another key to achieving buy-in is for the finance team itself to proactively inject core finance capabilities at all levels of the organization. This allows all members to plan, have better control and understanding, and optimize financial resources to deliver sustainable projects. At the same time, healthy conversations between the client strategy and finance teams will naturally be encouraged to strike a balance between client and business impact and get finance to actively support the business case.

I wish to tell you a true story. In an insurance company the CXO asked me how to know if the relationship with the CFO and his area was healthy, and I answered him with a question: "How many times a week are both teams (CX and Finance) actively talking about results, objectives, and aligning plans together? When you bring an experience project to a committee, and it has already been through finance eyes several times, they will naturally feel supportive and give you a "fast track". My recommendation is, make the financiers really feel so much "ownership" of the projects that they are motivated to defend them. Human nature will make us want to protect something we feel as our own, and that is what we should do with the finance team.

I know companies where this maxim reaches the point where the finance team itself seeks to constantly train the business areas in feasibility analysis (business case) so that they are not a bottleneck, and the various departments have more tools for self-management. Of course, this happens after a long road of trust. Let's not underestimate the importance of building bridges and creating internal strategic relationships; we can be surprised by what can be achieved by creating solid working team-blocks. That's why a CX strategist's best friend should be the financier.

Dimension 2: CX Economics Vision

Analyzes the clarity and degree of integration of the CX Economics vision in the company's culture and strategy. So, it implies that the organization recognizes and values the importance of the customer experience as a critical factor for long-term financial success. It also focuses on treating the customer experience as a strategic investment that generates an economic return. Companies should use storytelling techniques to support financial approval of projects where customer experience drives increased revenue through loyalty and retention, and thus genuinely promote the idea that it is more profitable to retain existing customers than to acquire new ones.

Another vital pillar in this dimension is for employees to understand the importance of CX by considering the customer lifecycle and the relationship between customer experience and long-term profitability, thus integrating this discipline into day-to-day conversations and planning.

Many will say that this point refers to the typical customer-centric vision, but it is not, because today this is no longer enough. Many companies make the mistake of seeking to generate a transformation of the experience, when the company is not ready, because most employees do not understand or feel in their daily lives how a better experience benefits the company, and obviously them. This is exactly what the CX

Economics vision must achieve, that is, to raise awareness in a real way of what tangible impacts are generated in the organization. I once asked a leader of a financial company: "Do you know how much a customer is worth? Do all employees have an estimate of this figure? Every employee should know that figure, as it is the only way for them to perceive how their work has an impact on increasing or decreasing that value.

Companies that are more advanced in this dimension have achieved that all employees (regardless of their area) understand customer value and become promoters and defenders of experience initiatives, and this in turn generates coherence in the organization's discourse, in which a long-term view is more important.

Dimension 3: Segmentation and Metrics Management

Examines the customer segmentation required to conduct CX Economics, which facilitates understanding how different sets of customers contribute to the company's financial performance and how improving the customer experience can affect overall profitability. Additionally, it evaluates how the company measures and manages CX and business metrics in each segment to assess the economic return produced by CX actions.

It is important to emphasize the relevance of identifying customer segments to understand how a better customer experience can affect the performance of different customer groups through the calculation of Customer Lifetime Value (CLTV). In this sense, the implementation and management of a robust VoC program that raises different measurement points is necessary to detect areas of improvement and monitor progress towards customer loyalty objectives.

In this case, unfortunately I have evidenced that companies make two mistakes. The first is that many organizations believe that it is enough to obtain empathy maps and personas, which are key to experience management, but in that state it is not useful for economic connection. Therefore, it is necessary to create what I call VALUE PERSONAS, a representation of a group of customers that also contains business and financial data and that is a real connection for the calculation of CLTV. For example, in an automotive company, the creation of value personas allowed us to have clarity on the monetary contribution of each customer group for both sales and post-sales, which even helped to calculate the financial absorption (KPI of the sector) by type of customer. I always mention that managing customer experience is important, but on top of that is customer strategy (which includes looking at our financial impacts throughout the customer lifecycle).

On the other hand, the second point is that companies underestimate the need to create a robust insights engine, which allows for experience, business, and operational metrics at all key touchpoints. Remember that there will be key touchpoints for experience (traditional measurement), but we will also need to measure other touchpoints that are decisive for business impact. These other elements are the most important for CX Economics. Are you measuring both in your company?

Dimension 4: Statistical, Analytical and Behavioral Tools

Evaluates the degree of sophistication and effectiveness with which a company uses various tools and techniques to collect, analyze and understand CX-related data to link customer experience and its impact on financial results.

For example, it is essential to apply principles of psychology and human behavior in understanding behavioral patterns that lead customers to take certain business actions, as well as to use advanced statistical tools to analyze data, obtain valuable information on trends that affect customer experience and perform validations that confirm certain hypotheses. In this context, sentiment analysis, text mining and natural language tools can also be used to understand customers' emotions towards the brand and their experiences.

Thus, the integration of various sources and techniques ensures a holistic view of the customer experience from a methodological point of view.

This is probably the most complex dimension because it requires specific talent, and often also certain technology (which is sometimes a barrier for smaller companies). But, it should not be a limitation, since you can start trying simpler tools and technology, and many times at no cost or low value. For me, this dimension differentiates companies that have a high level of maturity in the real financial management of the experience, as they make a genuine effort to develop new capabilities.

I remember a retail company I worked with that began a journey in building statistical, analytical and behavioral skills. I saw firsthand a before and after. The introduction of statistical tools and models made it possible to give greater robustness and depth to the analysis of experience data; and the use of quantitative methodologies made it possible to extrapolate the results to the customer base. Likewise, technology was implemented that allowed us to process more data in real time, and to create a more powerful and personalized close loop with AI. But, undoubtedly, the most powerful aspect was the infusion of behavioral techniques for the analysis, modeling, and monitoring of the impact on the business since this allowed us to link behavioral patterns with business data.

Dimension 5: ROI Impact & Project Scaling

Estimates how the company calculates and compares the return on its CX investments, identifying the economic value generated by each specific initiative. In addition, it analyzes how the company can successfully scale and replicate successful CX projects in different areas or segments of the organization for broader and sustainable impact by managing multiple projects at once.

The first thing is to demonstrate and achieve a solid understanding of the business and CX that allows us to develop a customized format to calculate the return on investment (ROI) for each CX initiative, as each sector, type of business and even project will have a different calculation model for the ROI of the experience (beyond the formula, the challenge lies in the calculation of the benefits).

However, the prioritization of projects must also be managed through a financial evaluation, other strategic variables and customer management that serve to give an order to the initiatives, implement them, manage them, and develop scaling plans (to those with a positive impact on ROI) to replicate them in different areas or segments of the organization.

I have seen that many companies focus on a static ROI analysis (a single project). The big problem with this is that organizations do not manage a single project, but must prioritize, decide, and manage several projects at once. So, this brings first the challenge of prioritizing which initiatives will be done and why.

Here we can happily use various Project Management tools that will help us align our list of top initiatives.

Each organization will have a way to prioritize, and that will depend on the factors and weights used for the objective. But the most complex is the management of assumptions that will obviously impact the number of benefits of each project. A healthcare company asked me to help them create a CX ROI model, and the first thing I told them was that generating the model was not the hard part (when you have the numbers, the data, and the right people it should flow smoothly), but rather that we should all agree on the assumptions. And in fact, it was, more than 50% of the project was in the generation of assumptions and scenarios, and in agreeing with all the areas involved. But once the assumptions were validated, running the model was simply easy, having the inputs at a glance.

The next challenge is to scale the initiatives, since generally when a project is implemented, it starts with a pilot or in a more controlled context. When organizations see results, they rush to scale it, not realizing that as they grow in scope, many of the assumptions of the model are not met. This is where many leaders lose faith or say, "it only worked because it was a pilot". Therefore, in this part it is vital to ensure that scaling up and/or replication on a larger scope maintains the initial assumptions, even though this implies more adjustment time. It is better to invest a little more time, but with a higher success rate.

Dimension 6: Financial Management Evaluation & Governance

Measures the company's ability to examine its financial statements and understand how the customer experience impacts bottom-line financial results. It assesses how the company uses financial information to identify opportunities and challenges related to customer experience, and how it uses this understanding to make informed decisions about CX strategies and resource allocation.

Therefore, various CX perspectives should be integrated into budgets and financial projections to make informed decisions at the strategic level, while generating an assessment of the financial impact of projects on the financial statements, considering investment, recurring expenses, cost savings, sales generated and expected EBITDA/net profit.

It is recommended to continuously monitor organizational results and the impact of CX actions to adjust in real time and ensure that strategies are aligned with financial objectives through a CX Balance Scorecard that allows dividing business objectives and financial goals into different levels and areas, assigning responsibilities, impacts and indicators for follow-up and compliance with the total financial result

Finally, senior management must have the ability to effectively communicate the results of the CX-related financial statement evaluation to all levels of the organization.

In this dimension I have experienced several times an "anti-finance" attitude. "I don't see finance in the company", "That's for the financial area to see", "I've already made sure I have a positive ROI, now it's Finance's turn" are some of the messages I have heard from CXOs. And here there is undoubtedly a serious mistake; the ROI calculation is necessary as a great first step of a business case, but as they would say in mathematics: "ROI is necessary, but not enough". We need to get to the bottom line of the business, to see the real benefit of our initiatives. While ROI is a commercial indicator, EBITDA (or whatever profit each company uses) is a financial indicator.

Some time ago I had a conversation with a leader of an entertainment company, and he always proudly gave me the ROI generated by "X" initiative. One day I asked him: "What is the additional benefit that "X" project brings to your bottom line? It is one thing for an initiative to bring us 150% ROI, or its equivalent in margin of USD 500,000. But it is another thing to bring us an additional 1.5% in EBITDA and to be able to see with "X-rays" exactly in which profit and loss statement accounting lines the great experience project we are managing impacts. Being able to move from a purely commercial ROI commentary to a financially focused EBITDA discussion automatically generates a strategic conversation. That is where our most important stakeholders will want to talk, and that will allow us to connect organizational objectives with actions, adjustments and initiatives that generate greater credibility.

Integrating the dimensions of the XQUEMA model

Before thinking about complex methodologies and calculations that do not lead us to a systematic way of linking experience to business results, CX leaders and professionals must understand that the only way to reach a true integral vision of experience as a discipline that has a direct and real impact on the last line of business is through the generation of a framework that gathers the necessary dimensions to achieve a task that is far from being only quantitative.

Thus, the question naturally arises: How advanced is my organization in each of the dimensions? The answer is an issue that will continue to evolve as awareness of the state of maturity of the financial management of the experience increases.

My intention is that by reading this chapter, you have been able to open your minds more to the real customer strategy with a long-term view of profit and not only quantitative but also qualitative management. In my experience, finance not only represents a way to monetize, but becomes an "act of confirmation of faith". The client experience has had an era of "believe to see" (let's invest and see what results will come...), but we now need an era of "see to believe" (smart investment and a consistent management with our client strategy). This is necessary taking into account that many transformations fail to consolidate results. That is why I am a firm believer that having a comprehensive financial approach to customer science will further professionalize this beautiful discipline. Let's always think that more than WOW, we must look for the ROW (Return on WOW).

About Sebastien Munar

Senior executive in the areas of customer experience, strategic marketing, digital transformation, innovation, churn, analytics, commercial planning and pricing. With solid financial and quantitative knowledge. Professional experience in international companies, in airlines, mass consumption, media & press, B2B, telecommunications, banking, tech, automotive, insurance and entertainment. Economist with MBA. Fluent in Spanish, English and French, and with advanced level of Portuguese. Certified Customer Experience Professional (CCXP).

Member of the Global Board of Directors of the Customer Experience Professionals Association (CXPA). Sebastien specializes in everything related to CX & Loyalty Economics, Customer Strategy and Organizational Adoption of Customer Centricity. He is a postgraduate professor, speaker, and consultant in several countries in Latin America, North America and Europe. He has developed different methodologies and frameworks throughout his career focused on customer strategy, retention, and customer lifecycle management.

Email *sebastien.munar@clientrika.com*

Website *www.clientrika.com*

Linkedin *https://www.linkedin.com/in/sebastienmunar/*

Instagram *https://www.instagram.com/clientrika/*

YouTube: *https://goo.su/NSpmH1*

Facebook *https://www.facebook.com/clientrika*

Spotify: *https://goo.su/vUF154W*

Organization Structure and Culture

Employee Experience - The Paired Tasting Menu

Sandra D. P. Thompson

The customer experience is most often dependent on the synergistic relationship between the manager and the employee, the 'employee experience'.

This chapter is unlike anything else written about employee experience.

It introduces you to a concept found in the finest restaurants, "The Paired Tasting Menu" - the curation of an experience delivered by the Chef and Sommelier (Part I) and gives you practical recommendations for each course (Part II).

<u>Part I</u>

The Paired Tasting Menu

The Paired Tasting Menu relies on the chef and sommelier (wine expert) working in harmony with one another to create an incredible experience for the diner. In the case of this chapter, the **chef** therefore **represents the manager, the sommelier represents the employee and together they present an incredible experience to the customer.** They complement each other. They are both responsible for the work relationship that makes a customer experience meaningful and often exceed the customer's expectations.

Figure 1: The chef and the sommelier create a remarkable experience for the diner.

Imagine The Paired Tasting Menu

A Tasting Menu, often referred to as a **'culinary adventure'** is a carefully crafted collection of several dishes in small portions served as a single meal. It's a specially curated dining experience which allows chefs to showcase their creativity and skill while offering diners a unique, memorable journey through an array of flavours and textures. A Tasting Menu is often **'paired'** with wine carefully selected by a skilled sommelier (wine expert) to create an incredible dining experience.

How to read the Paired Tasting Menu

The courses in the Paired Tasting Menu represent the high-level stages (courses) of the employee journey (shown in figure two) and each stage (course) offers suggestions of what the chef (manager) and the sommelier (employee) could do to make their relationship synergetic.

We have replaced the typical menu course names like canapé - dessert with the names of the employee journey. The Chef's tasting menu are in standard font, the pairing is in italics.

Figure 2: The stages in the Employee Journey are the courses in The Paired Tasting Menu.

Employee Experience - Tasting menu

Attract the right candidate

Get the JD right - ask for help and manage expectations.

Convince me

Ask meaningful questions to find out more about the candidate

Ask depth questions to explore the culture and potential fit between you and the business

Get me started

Invest in a meaningful welcome pack, make sure all devices are ready and support functions are available to help

Invite your boss to a conversation about expectations (the psychological contract)

Develop me

Listen

Create the environment to give valuable feedback

Nurture me

Do what you can to encourage psychological safety

Help others know what you need to feel psychologically safe

Energise me

Use Neopic Archetypes to understand what people need across your business

Act on the insight the Neopic Archetypes test results throughout your relationship

Support me

Encourage your staff when they move onto their next challenge. They will be an advocate for you and your team.

Share what you have learned about the role and how it might evolve for the next person

Wish me well

Consider a fond farewell rather than 'an exit from the business'

People will remember how you made them feel

Figure 3: The Paired Tasting Menu - there are suggestions for Chef and the Sommelier for each course. The result of the chef's creation and Sommelier's recommendation is a remarkable experience for the diner (customer)

<u>Part II</u>

Let's take a closer look at the contents of the Paired Tasting Menu (figure three) - here's where you'll find practical recommendations managers and employees can act on right away.

Attract the right candidate

Before you write the CX role job description, do your research. 8 out of 10 customer experience professionals report that the CX role they perform rarely resembles their job description. Speak to a small sample of existing CX professionals in communities like Women in CX https://womenincx.community/ if you're developing a new JD. They will validate your ideas and make suggestions. These people will not only know what you need, they may even know people who would be brilliant in the role!

If you're looking to fill a vacant role, make sure you have canvassed the view of the person leaving. They can recommend adjustments to reflect what they did and what they should have been doing.

Convince me

Prepare interesting questions for the interview which are designed to find out more about WHO the candidate is, rather than just focus on what they have done and testing their ability to complete the tasks associated with the role.

Here are some example questions: *

- What is your definition of success (and how might your view contrast to the view of your friends and family)?

- What is your definition of luck in a professional setting?

- What is the crazy big idea you would try in this role if you could not fail?

*Adapted from DOAC - Stephen Bartlett.

Think of the interview as an opportunity for you to work out if you'd enjoy this role.

Here are some examples of questions:

- *How are decisions made here?*

- *Describe the attitude towards learning from things that did not go to plan?*

- *If fairness was the most important thing for me to experience, to feel psychologically safe, how would we work together to achieve this?*

- *Imagine someone has been in this role for 12 months. Could you describe what success would look like for that person and for you as their manager?*

Get me started

Start as you mean to go on… (1) The new recruit is given access to all of the technology and devices they need to get started right away (2) Contacts in IT, HR and Finance record personalised welcome videos and arrange follow up meetings.

Never underestimate the value of the welcome pack given to the member of staff on their first day. You could include some gifts that reflect the insight gained from the interview (Cat treats if they told you they have a cat).

Initiating a conversation about expectations (also known as psychological contract) is a wise move in your first few weeks in role. Very few managers have this conversation, and it will help both of you work together confidently.

Here's a link to some additional, brilliant information on psychological contracts from CIPD: _https://bit.ly/4aAmuAi_

The next three stages (develop, nurture & energise) are at the heart of the employee journey. They are critical to the Paired Tasting Menu.

Develop me

Listen. Listen fiercely. As a manager, always ask open questions and ask how your staff are and how they are getting on. Have regular conversations with them about their tasks but most importantly how they feel about their progress, what they enjoy, what they would like to try and experiment with in their role.

Pay attention to the answers your staff give you. So much conflict is avoided when managers choose to listen to what is said, what's not said and how the body language and facial expression match (or not). When you listen, you give the other person significance.

Exchanging feedback is central to on-going development. In a healthy and progressive work relationship all team members should be ready and willing to offer everyone feedback which they think would be truly beneficial for them to hear. Here are some tips:

- *Give the feedback straight away if you can. The individual can quickly recall what has happened (and take corrective action if necessary).*

- *Use the SBI approach which means describe the **situation** you're giving feedback about. Describe the **behaviour**, because they might not be aware of how they show up. Then mention **impact**, which is the consequence of the behaviour.*

Nurture me

Employees must feel able to thrive. They need to feel psychologically safe. Psychological safety is not something a manager bestows onto their staff. Individuals decide how they feel but there are some behaviours you should consider practicing for the best chance of success:

a. Show your understanding:

i. Recap what's said to confirm a collective understanding, "What I think I heard you say was xxx"

ii. Avoid placing blame by saying something like 'why did you do this?' and focus on the solutions 'how can we work toward making sure this goes more smoothly next time?'

b. Be present:

Engage and focus on the conversation - turn off notifications and don't read emails if you are remote and close your laptop if you are face to face.

c. Use your interpersonal skills:

i. Express gratitude for contribution from the team

ii. Clearly communicate the purpose of ad hoc meetings scheduled outside the normal or regular sessions.

d. Involve others in decisions:

Make sure that any significant decision can be influenced by contribution and that it isn't a 'done deal' when you speak with your team about it.

There are short quizzes you can take to discover what you need to feel psychologically safe. The result of this test https://brainleadership.com/solution/safety-assessment/ will help to explain to others the types of behaviour that make you feel secure. This test is most powerful when individuals within a team exchange their results.

Energise me

Knowing the needs of the people in your business is the key to energising them. Look at *https://www.weareib.co/our-toolbox* - this is one part of the menu where both the manager and the employee would benefit from exchanging and understanding one another's results.

Support me

Ensure that the people who leave your team but stay in the business have good memories of their experience with you. A long tenure can be tarnished when moving to another team is not treated with compassion and encouragement. What you do from the point of receiving a request for a reference, a resignation and your colleague's last day… all matters.

Create an opportunity for a 'moving on chat' where you can share your reflections of the role both good and bad so that tweaks can be made for the new person coming in. Send these notes to your manager and to the HR team.

Wish me well

Focus your attention on the theme of a 'fond farewell' - what would this look like for the member of staff leaving the business whether the circumstances of their leaving were their choice or not. Speak to the member of staff. What would be the fond farewell for them? On their terms.

Picture yourself three years from the point of leaving the business. How do you want people to remember you? People will remember how you made them feel. You could use this statement to decide how you will show up in your final months in the role.

*****

This chapter invites you to think about the relationship between the employee and the manager and how this impacts the customer's experience. While the concept of the Paired Tasting Menu is far-fetched, it should give you some robust and practical recommendations you can act on right away. I intended to simply whet your appetite (sorry!) with some new, practical ideas.

About Sandra Thompson

Sandra Thompson is an independent customer and employee experience consultant. She is the Founding Director of The Ei Evolution. She is the first Goleman Emotional Intelligence Coach in the UK and 'Top Emotional Intelligence Voice' on Linkedin.

Sandra is a Fellow of the Chartered Institute of Marketing, she is a contributor on the CX Lead Advisory Board, a TEDx speaker, a Founding Member of Women in CX, a trainer and a lecturer on topics including people management and leadership, customer experience and emotional intelligence.

A regular guest on webinars, panel interviews and podcasts, Sandra also increasingly gives keynotes on topics ranging from empathy, leadership, EI in education, the way we work, remote work and of course, emotional intelligence in CX and EX.

Sandra believes that when we know how the brain works we are more likely to create stronger emotional connections between customers and employees and between colleagues too.

Email *sandra@eievolution.com*

Website *www.eievolution.com*

Linkedin *https://www.linkedin.com/in/cxeisandra/*

Organisation Structure and Culture

Debunking Customer Experience Myths & Understanding Their Realities

Faran Niaz

As I embark on crafting this significant chapter for CX5, my focus lies on contributing value to a book enriched with the collective wisdom of esteemed CX professionals and Gurus. Reflecting on my previous contribution to CX4, where I shared insights into elevating a bank from the 23rd to the No.1 position in the UAE, the positive reader feedback encouraged me.

This time, I aim to delve into my recent experiences as a CX consultant, uncovering the nuances and challenges faced during the last couple of years. Throughout this journey, I encountered various issues often labeled as CX Myths. Delving into these misconceptions, I recognized their potential to lead organizations astray in crafting CX strategies.

In this chapter, I will debunk the Top CX Myths and offer pragmatic insights to guide organizations towards a more realistic perspective:

CX MYTH: Customer Experience Equals Customer Service

The prevailing myth that customer experience is synonymous with customer service oversimplifies the broader and more intricate concept of customer experience.

Many tend to equate the two terms, assuming that providing excellent customer service encompasses the entirety of a positive customer experience. This misconception limits the scope of understanding, constraining customer experience within the confines of direct customer-company interactions. By viewing these terms interchangeably, organizations risk neglecting crucial elements that contribute to the overall customer journey.

Reality: Customer Service is a Component, not the Entire Concept of Customer Experience

This is a common misconception I experienced across many organizations I worked with. It is shockingly surprising that even though every organization now aloud advocate customer experience, they struggle to define the difference between Customer Experience and Customer Service and ironically, the lack of this simple clarity is at the Top management level.

In reality, while customer service is undeniably a crucial component of customer experience, it represents just one facet of the broader concept. Customer experience transcends the transactional aspects of customer service, beginning well before a customer makes a purchase or seeks assistance. The journey spans the entire customer lifecycle, encompassing pre-sale interactions, the actual purchase or service encounter, and post-service engagement. It's a comprehensive tapestry that weaves together all touchpoints, forming a holistic narrative of a customer's relationship with a brand.

Customer service, on the other hand, specifically pertains to the direct communication and assistance provided by a company to its customers. While an essential element, it is not the entirety of the customer experience. The holistic view of customer experience includes factors such as brand perception, product quality, user interfaces, and the emotional connection customers develop with a brand over time.

Recognizing this distinction is pivotal for organizations aiming to excel in customer experience, as it prompts a shift from merely providing good service to delivering a seamless and delightful end-to-end customer journey.

In conclusion, understanding that customer service is just one part of the broader customer experience is essential for organizations seeking to elevate their overall customer satisfaction and loyalty. Acknowledging the multifaceted nature of customer experience allows businesses to craft strategies that encompass every interaction, from the initial point of contact to ongoing engagement, fostering enduring customer relationships and brand advocacy.

CX MYTH: Achieving a Perfect NPS Score Means Your Customers Are Entirely Satisfied

The widespread misconception that a perfect Net Promoter Score (NPS) equates to absolute customer experience success is deeply ingrained in many organizations. NPS, a metric widely used to measure customer loyalty and satisfaction, is often regarded as the holy grail of customer experience assessment. The myth suggests that if your NPS is flawless, your customers are unequivocally satisfied, loyal, and likely to become brand advocates. This perception can lead to a singular focus on achieving that elusive 100 score, fostering the belief that perfection in NPS automatically translates to a flawless customer experience. However, this myth oversimplifies the intricate dynamics of customer satisfaction, potentially diverting attention from other crucial elements of a robust customer experience strategy.

Reality: NPS is Just One Measure; Comprehensive CX Success Involves a Holistic View of Customer Satisfaction and Loyalty

In reality, while a high Net Promoter Score is undoubtedly a positive sign, it is only one piece of the larger customer experience puzzle. Pinning the entirety of CX success on NPS can lead to a myopic understanding of customer satisfaction. The holistic view of customer experience success extends beyond a single metric, requiring organizations to consider a myriad of factors that contribute to a customer's overall journey. Genuine customer satisfaction involves examining touchpoints, understanding pain points, and ensuring consistent, personalized interactions across the entire customer lifecycle. A perfect NPS might indicate a likelihood of customers recommending a brand, but it doesn't encapsulate the entire spectrum of their experiences. Achieving comprehensive CX success demands a multifaceted approach that incorporates diverse metrics, qualitative feedback, and an ongoing commitment to refining and enhancing every aspect of the customer journey.

Does a 100 NPS mean highly satisfied customer? Does Loyalty mean satisfaction? Not always!

A loyal customer can be dissatisfied. My daughter is a hardcore Apple fan, and she would not use another phone but an iPhone. That's her loyalty. No other brand no matter what. However, her dissatisfaction with the latest iPhone15 with its initial flaws was evident and lead to her frustrations. Yet, her loyalty demanded that she back the flaws and stick to the branch she loves.

Similarly, in one of the Board meetings, I presented an NPS survey. The score was 100. A perfect score! Everyone asked me, great, but why am I sharing it? In reply, I loudly read the comments from the customers mentioned on the same survey as "I love the Bank. I have always banked with you and my generations to follow will too. We feel its our home. Here is my full score. For you as me being your loyal customer. Yet, over the past few months, I have seen a decline in your services especially from the Branch. The queues are getting longer and staff courtesy is declining"

CX MYTH: Customer Centricity Means Customers First and Employees Second

The pervasive myth surrounding customer centricity often misguides organizations into believing that prioritizing customers must come at the expense of employees. This suggests a hierarchical approach, implying that customer satisfaction is the sole driver of business success, relegating employee well-being and engagement to a secondary concern. The myth assumes that to achieve customer-centric goals, organizations must single-mindedly focus on customer needs, potentially neglecting the crucial role of motivated and satisfied employees.

Reality: Customer Centricity Encompasses Both Customers and Employees Equally

In reality, authentic customer centricity involves a harmonious balance between prioritizing both customers and employees. It rejects the notion of an either-or scenario, recognizing that the satisfaction of both stakeholders is interconnected and vital for sustainable success. Organizations committed to true customer centricity understand that exceptional customer experiences are intrinsically linked to the well-being and engagement of their employees. Engaged and content employees are more likely to deliver superior customer service, creating a positive cycle that reinforces both customer and employee satisfaction.

Customer centricity, far from being a zero-sum game, thrives when employees are valued as essential contributors to the customer experience. Recognizing the symbiotic relationship between customer and employee satisfaction, successful organizations prioritize creating a workplace culture that fosters employee engagement, empowerment, and development. Rather than compromising one for the other, organizations understand that a customer-centric approach is strengthened by investing in their employees.

The reality is that frontline employees play a pivotal role in shaping and delivering the desired customer experience. When employees feel valued, supported, and aligned with the organization's customer-centric vision, they become enthusiastic advocates for customer satisfaction. Organizations need to acknowledge that employees are not just instrumental in delivering customer service; they are integral to the entire customer journey. This holistic approach involves cultivating an organizational culture that appreciates the interconnectedness of customer and employee centricity, realizing that the success of one reinforces the success of the other.

CX MYTH: CX is Only About Resolving Customer Complaints

The common misconception surrounding Customer Experience (CX) is the belief that it primarily revolves around addressing and resolving customer complaints. This myth stems from the notion that the essence of CX lies solely in reactive measures to rectify issues raised by customers. While resolving complaints is undeniably a crucial aspect of customer service, constraining CX within this narrow scope overlooks the broader dimensions that contribute to a comprehensive customer experience strategy.

Reality: CX Encompasses the Entire Customer Journey

In reality, Customer Experience extends far beyond merely addressing complaints. It encapsulates the entirety of the customer journey, starting from the initial point of interaction and spanning through each touchpoint. Proactive measures, personalized interactions, and creating positive moments throughout the entire lifecycle are integral components of a holistic CX strategy. Exceptional CX involves understanding customer needs, anticipating their expectations, and actively engaging with them at various stages, not just when issues arise.

While addressing complaints is crucial, focusing solely on eactive problem-solving neglects opportunities to elevate the customer experience during positive interactions. Brands that excel in CX understand that fostering loyalty and satisfaction involves consistently exceeding customer expectations, whether through personalized communication, streamlined processes, or anticipating needs before they become complaints.

Moreover, the myth tends to position CX as a departmental responsibility rather than a company-wide commitment. In reality, every department, from marketing and sales to product development, contributes to the overall customer experience. Creating a customer-centric culture requires collaboration across the organization, emphasizing that CX is not the sole domain of the customer service team.

Dispelling the myth allows organizations to recognize that proactive CX initiatives contribute significantly to building brand loyalty and positive perceptions. By integrating customer-centricity into every aspect of the business, companies can forge stronger connections with customers, foster brand advocacy, and differentiate themselves in a competitive market.

CX MYTH: CX is Different for B2C and B2B

The prevailing myth suggests that Customer Experience (CX) strategies should be fundamentally different for Business-to-Consumer (B2C) and Business-to-Business (B2B) companies. This misconception assumes that the nature of the customer relationship, purchasing dynamics, and touchpoints in these two realms requires entirely distinct CX approaches. While there are nuances, treating B2C and B2B CX as entirely disparate endeavors oversimplifies the complexity of customer interactions in both contexts.

Reality: Common Principles Underlie B2C and B2B CX

In reality, the core principles of CX are remarkably similar across B2C and B2B landscapes. Both involve understanding customer needs, providing value, and delivering positive experiences. While the dynamics may differ, the underlying goal remains the same: to create satisfied, loyal customers. B2C and B2B customers, despite their different roles and decision-making processes, share common expectations such as prompt service, transparency, and personalized interactions.

Acknowledging the similarities enables organizations to leverage successful CX practices across both B2C and B2B environments. For instance, principles like proactive communication, anticipating customer needs, and building strong relationships are universally applicable. B2B transactions may involve more complex decision-making units, longer sales cycles, and deeper relationships, but the fundamental desire for a positive customer experience is inherent in both scenarios.

By adopting a holistic CX approach that integrates the best practices from both B2C and B2B, organizations can create a seamless and consistent customer experience strategy. The focus should be on understanding the specific needs and pain points of customers within each context while recognizing the shared principles that contribute to overall satisfaction.

CX MYTH: Experience in CX is Industry Biased

I had to add this one based on my personal experiences. The prevailing myth suggests that expertise in Customer Experience (CX) is inherently tied to specific industries, creating a belief that insights gained in one sector, such as banking, may not be applicable or transferable to others like hospitality, telecom, or aviation. This misconception assumes that CX knowledge is siloed and cannot transcend industry boundaries. In my personal experience as a consultant with 25 years in banking, I several times encountered the perception that my CX insights were only relevant within the financial sector, limiting their application elsewhere.

Reality: CX Principles Transcend Industries

Contrary to the myth, the reality is that CX principles are fundamentally universal and can be adapted across diverse industries. While industry nuances exist, the core tenets of understanding customer needs, delivering personalized experiences, and fostering customer loyalty are applicable across the board. My consulting journey allowed me to debunk this myth as I successfully applied CX strategies from banking to hospitality, telecom, and aviation. The key lies in recognizing the common thread of customer-centricity that runs through all industries and tailoring approaches to suit specific contexts. True expertise in CX is not confined by industry; rather, it is rooted in a deep understanding of customer behavior and the ability to adapt proven strategies to various business landscapes.

The CX world needs to understand this, a CX expert of one Industry is equally if not more, adequately capable of running CX strategy and implementation for any Industry.

About Faran Niaz

Faran Niaz is Director Customer Experience for HALA based in Riyadh, Saudi Arabia and Dubai , UAE.

He is also CEO & Founder of 'CX Future' where it's all about Customer Experience. His passion is working with organizations to help develop a culture that ensures not just for customers to come back, customer retention, but to create deeply loyal customers. Making a difference in terms of how organizations approach a customer and how they deliver great & exceptional experiences. Helping organizations to create that kind of a magnitude of experience that helps enhance their CX to maximize ROI & STAR Ratings.

Faran Niaz is listed amongst the 'Top 100 Global CX thought Leaders' and is also the co-author of the bestselling 'Customer Experience 4 – CX4'. He has over 25 years experience as an accomplished Customer Experience, Customer Centricity, employee engagement and change management expert with some of the top financial Institutions in the world including Citibank, Mashreq & ADIB. He has been an architect of winning multiple CX awards and creating a unique record of moving one of the Banks in UAE from 23rd to No.1 Bank in Customer Experience and maintaining it for record 7 consecutive years. He is an Internationally recognized Motivation & Keynote Speaker and Awarded by 'Awards International' as the most experienced 'CX Judge' chairing over 30 events globally.

Faran is also an Award winning Photographer with his work exhibited in Italy, Thailand, United Arab Emirates and Pakistan.

LinkedIn *https://www.linkedin.com/in/farann/*

Email *farannniaz@yahoo.com*

Website *fniaz@HALA.com*

Organisation Structure and Culture

Learnings from the State of Customer-Centricity Project

Jonathan Daniels

Lots of organisations are waking up to the power of Customer Experience. More and more leaders are quoted saying: "We need to put our customers at the centre of everything we do". This is the idea of installing a customer-centric culture within an organisation. But how easy is it to be customer-centric? We know the phrase sounds nice, and we know it's very much in fashion. But what does it really mean to be customer-centric? We set out to demystify the meaning of customer-centricity. Considering we spend so much of our lives at work, and considering that over the last few years customer-centric companies seem to perform better than the rest. If we can work out the ingredients of a customer-centric organisation, then we can replicate this with other organisations.

Before we begin, I must mention that customer-centricity is a not a straight forward topic. Customer-centicity is about culture and organisational behaviour, and those who lead culture transformations have had a hard time throughout the years. They have often been criticized for having inconsistent definitions and terminology. Also there is generally a dubious connection to business results, and overall a history of wasting time and money and leaving problems unresolved. If that's not enough their actions are often considered too much on the side of 'soft management', to the point that there is nothing substantial in what they do. For example, they often do not really offer a clear method to measure progress.

Luckily I was not tackling this challenge alone. Firstly I have Bongani Ncube to help me with this task. And in addition, at CX Centric we have built a global community of people like me who work within the Customer Experience field. And as such we were able to call on a number of practitioners from around the world to give feedback, opinions and their views on the matter. Some of those practitioners have also written chapters in this book.

After a lot of 'tooing' and 'froing' midway through 2022 we published the first version of the CX Centric Customer Centricity Model. It had been refined following feedback from over 20 customer experience practitioners from around the world. Since then over 300 organisations from over 40 countries have used our model to assess their level of customer centricity. This allowed us to create a global benchmark around Customer Centricity. It has also allowed us to understand the beliefs, priorities and challenges of the average customer experience practitioner. But before this, let's look at how Customer Experience leaders define Customer-Centricity.

What does Customner-Centricity mean to you and your organisation?

The definition of Customer-Centricity is always controversial. The phrase can often mean different things to different people. Getting clarity and consensus for your organization is a critical success factor in your Customer Centric transformation.

Only 5% of organizations believe that Customer-Concentrity is about living by the mantra 'The Customer is always right.'

Just over half of organizations view Customer-Concentricity as a strategy to better understand who their customers are and how to meet their needs.

As well as thinking about the impact on customers in everything they do.

55%	Customer-centricity is understanding who our customers are, and how best to meet their needs.
55%	Customer-centricity is always thinking about the impact on our customer in everything we do
34%	Customer-centricity is focusing on the customer journey, and using this as a starting point for innovation.
33%	Customer-centricity is a strategic way to improve relationships with out customers
31%	Customer-centricity is a strategy to grow our business
5%	Customer-centricity is living by the mantra "The customer is always right."

When I entered into the world of customer experience I did so because it was my belief that having a better understanding of the Customer would lead to more productive employees. I thought to myself that if we could help teams to understand things from the customers perspective, then they would be able to make better decisions as they go about their daily activities.

In the case that you are one of the leaders I previously mentioned who have stated 'we want our organisation to be customer-centric', a good idea is to set a clear definition about what customer-centricity actually means. So we asked: 'What does Customer-Centricity mean to you and your organisation'. And we learn that: 'Understanding who our customers are and how to meet their needs' and 'always thinking about the impact on our customer in everything we do' were the most popular answers. Does this resonate with you?

Only 5% of organisations believe that customer-centricity is about living by the mantra: 'The Customer is always right'. This phrase was famously promoted by Harry Gordon Selfridge, the founder of the Selfridges department store which was first established in London, UK. He famously said "The customer is always right—until proven wrong." It seems that this phrase has been replaced, the average opinion has changed. Yet Selfridges lives on and continues to outperform other retail stores.

Below I have outlined the CX Centric Customer Centricity Model. It has a total of 8 dimensions, and each dimension consists of 3 sub-dimensions. As this is a short essay we focus on the principle 8 dimensions. We will walk through each of them individually:

- Customer Vision and Strategy

- Customer-Centric Leadership

- Experience Design & Innovation

- Technology & Insights

- Customer-Centric Community

- Employee Experience

- Measurement & Performance

- Continuous Learning & Improvement

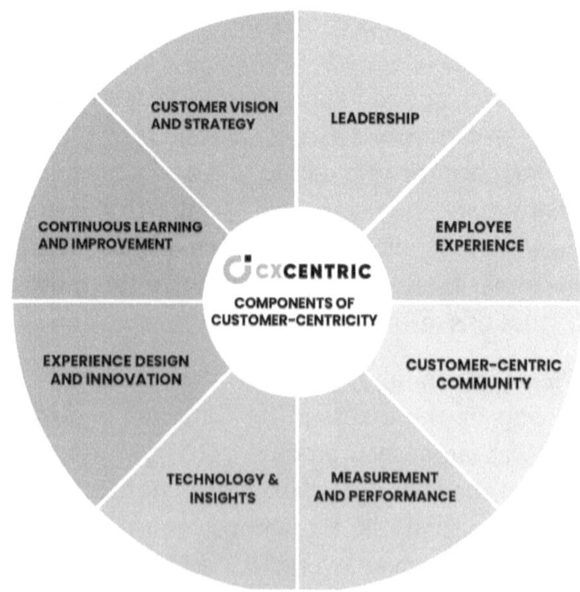

Customer Vision and Strategy

Establishing a Customer Experience (CX) vision is pivotal for organizations aiming to foster a customer-centric culture. Firstly, it creates a clear direction for all employees, aligning their efforts toward a unified goal of delivering exceptional experiences. This shared vision serves as a guiding beacon, ensuring that every aspect of the organization, from product development to customer support, is geared towards customer satisfaction. As Henry Wadsworth Longfellow, the famous American poet once said: "In the long run men hit only what they aim at".

A well-defined CX vision is a potent tool for brand differentiation, providing a sustainable competitive advantage. In a crowded market, where products and services can be similar, the way a brand treats its customers can be a key differentiator. This not only attracts customer loyalty but also enhances the brand's reputation.

Moreover, a compelling CX vision attracts commitment and increases employee motivation. When employees understand the significance of their role in shaping positive customer experiences, they become more engaged and motivated, contributing to a positive work environment. The establishment of a CX vision sets a standard of excellence, guiding employees on the target experience.

Customer-Centric Leadership

Customer-centric leadership is a critical success factor for customer-centric culture. As the great Mary Kay Ash once said: "The speed of the leader is the speed of the gang". It begins with an acknowledgement and respect for the importance of the customer's experience, signified by budget and resources allocated to Customer Experience related initiatives. Our research shows that 60% of leaders do not invest enough resources in their Customer Experience. Without the required investment the initiatives are bound to fail before they have even started.

Effective leaders lead from the front and lead by example.

Customer-centric leaders are also transparent in what they say and do, and they are authentic. In order to take their employees on a journey with them, they know that they need to encourage and nurture a passion for customer experience. So this means communicating with employees and connecting with them on a human level. This is a lot more that setting KPIs for the business. This is genuinely communicating about the customer challenges and goals, and making a case about where the organisation makes a difference in customers' lives.

Experience Design & Innovation

A customer-centric organisation designs experiences that its customers appreciate. In order to do this of course they must define the experience. But also they must have a clear design process. Successful companies tend to ensure that their experiences are generally aligned, and this requires a strong internal process. Today we notice that many organisations suffer due to a clash between those managing the product, and those managing the experience. Those managing the product often sit in the IT department and manage a strong budget. Whereas the people managing customer experience often sit in the marketing department and need to negotiate with product owners regarding priorities. Sir Jonathan "Jony" Paul Ive was Chief Design Officer at Apple. He oversaw the release of many well known Apple products including the iPod, iPhone, iPad, and the MacBook. He was famously quoted saying: "The design process is about designing and prototyping and making. When you separate those, I think the final result suffers". Customer-centric organisations incorporate customers and customer feedback into the design process. They understand that real innovation is a result of trying and testing, and give their employees space to do just that.

Technology & Insights

Today a lot of customers experience brands through digital channels. Digital experiences present an opportunity to organisations, because they generate data which can be used to further improve the experience, as well as opportunities to ultimately sell more.

Harnessing data to design experiences is paramount for organizations seeking factual insights over opinions. By relying on data, businesses can drive higher profits through customer expansion, leveraging accurate information for strategic decision-making. The process uncovers valuable opportunities more frequently, allowing companies to refine their offerings. Furthermore, a data-centric approach supports the delivery of personalized experiences, enhancing customer satisfaction and loyalty. Beyond the customer-centric benefits, it also reduces costs associated with manual data analysis. Additionally, the sharing of insights across functions improves organizational alignment, fostering a collaborative environment where departments can work cohesively based on a shared understanding of data-driven perspectives. In essence, prioritizing data-driven design not only enhances customer relationships but also streamlines internal processes for overall organizational success.

Customer-Centric Community

A customer-Centric community is a network of colleagues across the organization that meet regularly to discuss customer trends and to identify how to improve the customer experience. They collaborate and support each other to implement improvements to the Customer Experience and drive business growth. They collaborate with customers directly to bring in the outside-in perspective, and are committed to ensuring that the voice of the customer is heard and considered throughout the organisation.

The majority of medium and large organisations today suffer

from misalignment between teams, resulting in organisational silos. This is where different teams compete against each other, or operate independently, rather than work towards a collective goal. A customer-centric community is a very strong tool to bridge the gap between silos. By uniting teams around customer personas, key customer journeys and feedback from customers, we are able to bring employees together to solve customer problems collectively.

Employee Experience

By now the majority of leaders we speak to understand that in order to deliver great experiences, we must begin with the employee experience. As Max Lucado said: 'A man who wants to lead the orchestra must turn his back on the crowd'. Prioritizing employee experience is vital for organisational success on multiple fronts. Enhancing employee satisfaction and loyalty directly contributes to a positive work environment, boosting overall morale. This, in turn, has a ripple effect on customer experience, as satisfied employees are more likely to deliver exceptional service. Improved employee engagement and contentment elevate productivity, encouraging more efficient work practices. Moreover, by tapping into the collective wisdom of employees, organizations can align their workforce toward achieving set goals and objectives. Investing in employee experience not only increases the lifetime value of employees but also establishes a consistent approach to managing change. Ultimately, fostering a positive employee experience is a strategic investment that positively influences various aspects of organizational performance, from productivity to customer satisfaction.

Measurement & Performance

Measuring business performance is an essential practice for any team. As Peter Drucker the great Management thought leader said: "If you can't measure it, you can't change it". When measuring performance customer-centric organisations include measurements from the customers' perspective. So using KPIs such as Net Promoter Score, Customer Satisfaction (CSAT) and Customer Effort Score (CES). But in addition they work hard to understand factors driving customer sentiment and customer behaviour. They want to understand the reason behind the scores that customers provide.

Customer-centric metrics provide strong direction for employees by pinpointing areas that require attention. It answers the question: "are we on the right path" and can help to identify early warning signs.

Continuous Learning & Improvement

Many successful leaders of today have often highlighted the importance of having a growth mindset. This is where you consider learning a 'win' in itself. Continuous Learning and improvement is a multilevel process where members individually and collectively acquire knowledge by acting together and reflecting together. The survival of any organisation today depends to a large extent on how well it can adapt to environmental changes, respond to change, and operate more effectively. All these tasks require the organization to learn continuously. Customer-centric organisations expand their syllabus to ensure they are learning about more efficient ways of working, changes related to society and the environment, and aof course customer needs. An organisation which stays up to date around emerging customer needs will put themselves in a position to be able to serve them better. 28% of people we surveyed know how their business impacts society and the environment, and they are passionate about it.

Conclusions

Overall in this essay we present the CX Centric Customer Centricity model which has now been used by over 300 organisations around the world. We notice that organisations with the ambition of competing on customer experience are facing similar challenges wherever they are in the world. This model serves as a tool to help measure a team or organisations level of customer centricity. And we are confident that organisations which excel in these eight diciplines will create the right environment within their organisations and equip their employees to create differentiated experiences which will lead to happier customers and ultimately higher profits.

About Jonathan Daniels

Jonathan has a focus of improving Customer Experience as a practice, as well as supporting and educating others on the topic.

He is the author of The Customer Experience Playback.

He has founded successful communities including CX Brussels, CX Dubai and the global CX Centric network. He also is the author of the Customer Centricity Maturity Model and the State of Customer Centricity Project.

He runs CX Centric, a successful Customer Experience consultancy.

Linkedin: *https://www.linkedin.com/in/jdaniels-cx/*

Twitter: *cxcentricglobal*

Instagram: *cxcentric*

Organisation Structure and Culture

How Top-Performing Boards Can Influence Highly Effective Customer Engagement Leading To Positive Growth.

Eng. Ahmed Alfaddagi

Introduction

As practitioners in the customer experience (CX) domain, we recognize the significant impact of our efforts on shaping customers' perceptions throughout their journey with our organizations. This journey, originating from our brand's promises, encompasses a series of emotions and decisions. Our aim is to create a positive experience, thereby increasing customer satisfaction, loyalty, and advocacy. Crucially, these customer-centric efforts yield tangible ROI by enhancing customer lifetime value, reducing churn, and lowering customer acquisition costs. Ultimately, this elevates overall profitability and enhances the returns on our CX investments.

As the highest supervisory authority, the Board of Directors (BoD) bears overall responsibility for the strategic direction of an organization. They fashion organizational culture through their beliefs and mindset, and this permeates throughout the entire organization. They are, therefore, influencing the customer experience that their organization is delivering, and I believe that proactive engagement in this realm is fundamental to the organization's pursuit of success and sustainable growth.

Despite its importance, many find themselves inadequately engaged with the strategic aspects of CX. Drawing on insights from best practices and diverse interactions, this chapter explores the challenges and barriers that hinder BoDs from effective CX engagement and offers a framework for strategic engagement in CX.

The Challenge: A Disconnect Between Intent and Action

A Harvard study surveyed 30 large US companies, revealing that over one-third reported their boards spend less than 10% of their time discussing marketing or customer-related issues [1]. Furthermore, a PwC case study showed that less than 25% of directors engage in direct interactions with customers. Another indicator, from the latest McKinsey Quarterly global surveys, found that only about 20% of directors feel they fully grasp their company's strategy, including CX aspects [2]. These trends suggest that shareholder interests and regulatory mandates related to governance and finance predominantly dictate the BoD's meeting agendas and discussions.

This lack of BoD engagement in CX strategically can have dire consequences. This is not just about missing opportunities; it's a significant risk, especially in an era where customer-centricity is crucial for organizational growth and sustainability. Therefore, BoDs need to take a greater interest in CX than many currently do.

Organizational Culture and Customer Experience

The organizational culture exists regardless of our awareness; it continuously and interactively forms itself. It encompasses various elements, including individual and collective mindsets, norms, beliefs, and values. These elements manifest in observable norms, articulated opinions, and demonstrable behaviors, creating a cycle that continuously shapes and reshapes these cultural drivers in wide-ranging and durable ways.

An adaptive and dynamic culture is crucial for the BoD to ensure the organization's customer experience (CX) efforts are both progressive and permanent. The BoD plays a pivotal role in developing and reinforcing this culture, employing both top-down and bottom-up approaches. By setting a top-level tone, they influence the adoption of best practices in CX. Simultaneously, their indirect support for a bottom-up approach empowers employees to contribute actively to the cultivation of a customer-centric culture.

1. Bringing Customers into the Boardroom, Harvard Business Review

2. Does a Customer on the Board of Directors Affect Business-to-Business Firm Performance?, Journal of Marketing

Barriers to Effective BoD CX Eengagement

Lack Of Role Clarity

Numerous board members perceive their primary role as focusing on regulatory compliance and financial maximization. This narrowed perspective often leads to diminished engagement in key areas, including CX-related matters.

Lack Of CX Focus In Board Agendas

Although the BoD might recognize their role in CX, their agendas are predominantly occupied with financial reviews and compliance matters, leaving minimal time and focus for CX discussions. More metric's, and KPIs around CX need to be in place because by tracking it, you will manage performance improvement in this space.

Lack of CX Information and knowledge

A significant barrier is the limited CX information available to board members, as well as an understanding of the components of CX, and it is not just about complaint handling. Typically, they receive extensive reports focused on financial data, yet these often lack vital details on CX metrics, customer insights, and the competitive landscape. This dearth of crucial information hinders the board's ability to engage with and make well-informed decisions regarding CX topics.

Dysfunctional Boardroom Dynamics

The fourth one is dysfunctional boardroom dynamics that cover different forms in the board compositions and members' attitudes. Even when board members have reservations about the company's CX strategy or operational topics, they may hesitate to speak up due to a lack of industry knowledge or fear of conflict. Accordingly, this holds back the open discussion and hinders the board's ability to guide the organization effectively in the CX issues.

Framework For Effective BoD CX Engagement

Having seen this so many times and also worked to/with many Boards to remedy these challenges, I have established a framework that I will share with you.

The proposed framework for Boards of Directors (BoD) to engage effectively in customer experience includes the BoD CX Engagement Model alongside roles and practices facilitating this engagement. This framework, derived from my experiences in enhancing BoD effectiveness and emphasizing the importance of CX in maximizing organizational value, is crucial.

Early establishment and customization of this framework and the CX Governance Model are key in clarifying the relationships and interconnections within the organization's CX ecosystem and the ongoing success of BoD practices.

BoD Effective CX Engagement Model

The Effective Customer Experience Engagement Model for the BoD encompasses several interrelated components. These are illustrated in Figure 1 and include:

1. BoD CX Mindset.

2. CX Value-Creation Enablement (CX strategy, people, policies and Processes, and CX technology).

3. CX Interaction Ecosystem (CX Culture and Knowledge Management).

4. Balanced BoD Value Practices.

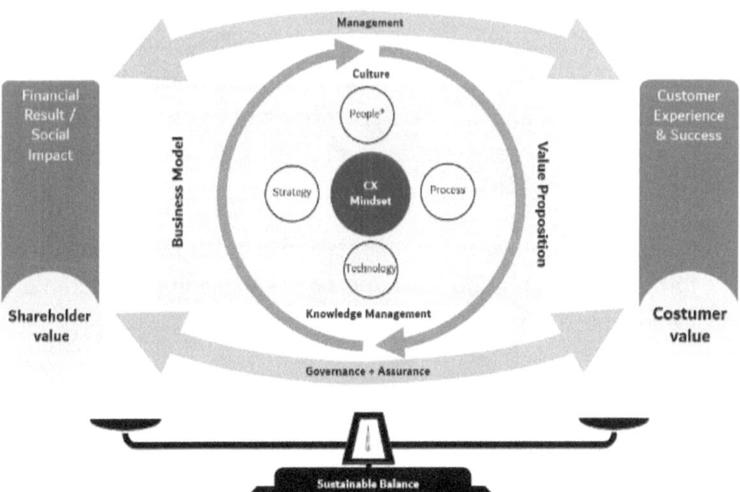

Figure 1: BoD Effective CX Engagement Model

1. The BoD CX Mindset

The BoD CX mindset is the core of this model and consists of traits that strengthen the ability of both the BoD and the organization to make decisions and appraise problems, solutions, people, and reality toward customers.

The important aspect of this mindset is the actionable dimension compared to the attitude dimension, where all organizational efforts should progress in all CX capabilities. The prominent BoD CX engagement mindset traits are:

- Customer-centric, whereby the BoD always prioritizes customer needs in decision-making processes.

- Curious, board members should ask insightful questions about customer behaviors, preferences, and feedback to gain a deeper understanding, which can be invaluable for CX strategy and other related operational interactions.

- Collaborative, board members should be willing to collaborate in the board room with other members and with the stakeholders, key customers, and internal departments to ensure a unified approach to customer experience, minimizing or removing isolated information and efforts in any part of the organization.

- Decisiveness, whereby BoD adapts and encourages making informed decisions about customers quickly to enhance customer value proactively.

2. CX Value-Creation Enablement:

The other main component in this model is the CX value-creation enablement, encompassing CX strategy, people, processes, and technology. The synergy among these components relies on a well-designed CX organization and operating model, which forces a seamless cross-functional collaboration to realize the defined CX ambitions and fulfill branding promises.

The first part of this component is the CX strategy. This strategy serves as a bridge linking the customer value proposition (CVP), as articulated in the enterprise business model and integral to the overarching enterprise strategy, with the aforementioned enablement components. The goal of the CX strategy is to develop and execute a comprehensive plan, ensuring the effective communication of the CVP through the organization's delivery mechanisms.

The people component in this model includes the organizational leadership of BoD, C-suits, and the rest of the organization's employees. Human capital is a critical enabler in providing a distinct experience to the organization's customers.

The policies and processes are the mechanical components that enable the employees to interact and utilize the other resources within the governance model and guidelines. Lastly is the technology component that plays a dramatic role nowadays in facilitating seamless interaction and maximizing the CX outcomes.

3. CX Interaction Ecosystem:

A culture driven by CX and effective knowledge management practices forms the foundation for CX value-creation enablement. This includes CX strategy, people, policies, processes, and technology. Together, these elements help to foster and deliver the customer value proposition effectively and efficiently.

4. Balanced BoD Value Practices: Governance, Management & Assurance

In general, management, governance, and assurance practices are key activities of BoD and the leadership team, ensuring the effective performance of this model in alignment with the organization's strategy. The extent of the BoD's involvement in these practices is strategic, influenced by contextual regulations and the organization's maturity in CX practices. A crucial consideration is achieving a balance between customer and financial value. This balance is essential to maximize sustainable value for shareholders while fulfilling the brand's promises to its customers.

The key area of the Board of Directors interaction with Customer Experience

Strategic Dimension: BoD should set standards and criteria and make strategic decisions that improve the customer experience.

Moreover, the BoD ensures that the organization's CX strategy aligns with its overall business objectives. This involves reviewing and approving the CX strategy, with a focus on its customer-centricity and its potential to drive value.

CX Governance Model: In the CX Governance Model, the board should either establish a specialized sub-committee for customer experience or define explicit CX-related roles within existing committees. Continuously monitoring regulatory changes is crucial. The board must also ensure regular audits of CX processes to maintain compliance.

Organizational Culture: BoD must exert influence over the key drivers and motivators that foster a vibrant, customer-focused culture. Moreover, they are responsible for establishing a tone that values customer-centricity at the highest level, ensuring that this mindset permeates through every layer of the organization.

Institutional Resources: They should allocate and direct the necessary institutional resources to manage customer experience effectively. This includes approving budgets and resources encompassing human resources, technology, and financial investments specifically earmarked for CX initiatives.

Human capital: The BoD plays a vital role in nurturing and incentivizing the organization's human capital to enhance customer experience efforts. It is imperative for the board to create an environment that fosters excellent customer experience management practices. Additionally, the board should measure employee experience strategically in the level of policies and the outcomes that impact the customer journey.

Policies and Processes: The board plays a vital role in guiding customer experience management efforts by adopting the relevant policies and guiding principles. Their strategic involvement extends beyond optimizing individual touchpoints to enhancing the overall customer journey.

Institutional Performance: Supervision and performance monitoring form a critical part of the board's role in customer experience management. This includes reviewing customer experience metrics, holding the executive team accountable for meeting these benchmarks, and scrutinizing the integrity and quality of the underlying data.

Technological Investments: The BoD must endorse technological investments that boost the customer experience. Additionally, they should explore the potential of emerging technologies, such as AI and blockchain, to further elevate CX initiatives.

Innovation and Customizations: The board has a critical role in ensuring that the customer value proposition stays relevant and responsive to changing customer needs and market offerings. Adopting a mindset of innovation and customization, along with implementing supportive policies and processes, is essential for organizations to adapt and meet customer requirements effectively.

The Key Practices Of The Board Of Directors For Effective CX Engagement

Understanding and building adaptive CX Strategy:

This process begins with the board comprehending Customer Value Proposition(CVP) from the customer's perspective. Key questions to address include:

1. What customer needs are we targeting, and what is our proposed solution?

2. How do we identify the most critical features and benefits for our customer segments?

3. How do we differentiate ourselves from our competitors in CX?

4. What steps are necessary to make our CX strategy profitable?

5. What is our plan for sustaining or renewing our competitive advantage in CX?

Then, build a robust CX strategy that involves several core elements: First, articulate a purpose and shared vision that aligns with the company's brand-value proposition. Second, developing a clear CX strategy map outlining strategic objectives related to CX from various perspectives (as illustrated in Figure 2). Third, identifying strategic initiatives to address gaps in the change agenda. Lastly, CX metrics should be established to be included in the Board's CX scorecard.

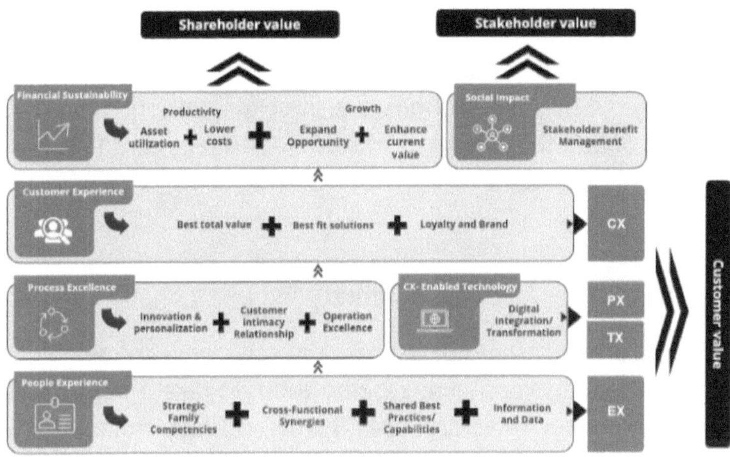

Figure 2: Generic CX Strategy Map

Regular CX Strategy Reviews:

The BoD should regularly review the organization's CX strategy. These reviews must consider the organization's context, maturity, and market presence to ensure alignment with business objectives and customer needs.

CX Performance Audits:

The board should periodically evaluate CX performance metrics to gauge the effectiveness of current initiatives and identify areas for improvement. This should be part of the board's monitoring function, and essential components of these audits should include:

- Incorporating a CX strategic information brief and updates in each board meeting book.

- Dedicating time during regular board meetings for updating and discussing CX issues

- Employing the CX Strategy Map to have a dedicated BoD CX Scorecard.

Stakeholder Engagement:

This includes key customers and a representative group of employees. Such interactions are vital for gathering insights that can shape the execution of the CX strategy and influence operational aspects.

Summary

Whilst I am not asking BoDs to do the actual work of delivering customer engagement, I am asking them to take more interest by having it on their agenda. The risk of not doing this is clear – by delivering a bad CX, you risk losing market share to your competitors. Price won't matter. Customers will pay for what they believe is a better CX. By using the principles in the framework that I have shared, you will definitely be able to have a positive change in your organization. As the highest supervisory authority, the Board of Directors (BoD) bears overall responsibility for the strategic direction of an organization, and, therefore, for the positive future of your organization, I invite you to take steps to drive a better CX.

About Ahmed Alfaddagi

Eng. Ahmed Alfaddagi is an experienced executive and thought leader with over two decades of diverse management experience, specializing in Customer Experience (CX), Strategic Planning, and Governance/Risk/Compliance (GRC) Management. As a Strategic Advisor in a number of government agencies and Senior Partner at a number of consulting firms, Ahmed has had a significant impact on the formulation and implementation of numerous strategic initiatives affecting the organizations he is affiliated with. Additionally, he is the Regional Leader of the KSA Chapter of the CXPA, which strengthens his influence in the CX domain.

Recent achievements of Ahmed are a result of his participation in numerous National Strategies and strategic plans for the Vision 2030 Program. His contributions to realizing Saudi Arabia's Vision 2030 Programs have spanned multiple sectors, including finance and non-profit organizations.

LinkedIn *https://www.linkedin.com/in/ahmedalfaddagi/*

Get Customer Experience 1-4

The bestselling Customer Experience (CX) series is available worldwide on Amazon.com. Here are the links below.

Customer Experience 1 https://amzn.to/2LmB0BZ

Customer Experience 2 https://amzn.to/3r9IBpX

Customer Experience 3 https://amzn.to/

Customer Experience 4 https://amzn.to/

Would You Like To Contribute To Future Editions of Customer Experience?

Customer experience as a professional is growing and evolving on a daily basis. There are many examples of innovative thinking and projects that have made a huge difference around the world.

The idea of this book is to allow CX practitioners around the world to share their best-practice stories for the mutual benefit of everyone.

All four outings of Customer Experience have been #1 international best-ranked, bestsellers in the categories of Customer Service, Customer Relations, Customer Experience Management, Consumer Behaviour and Marketing and Sales.

Clearly, professionals want to stay right up-to-date with what's happening in Customer Experience Management (CXM).

That's why we are actively looking for new contributors for our next edition of Customer Experience. If you are a CX professional and would like to get involved in the next release, then get in touch. All you need a good story to share that you know will add value to the readership.

If you would like to express your interest please contact Naeem Arif.

Naeem@NAConsulting.co.uk